The
Power of a
Dream

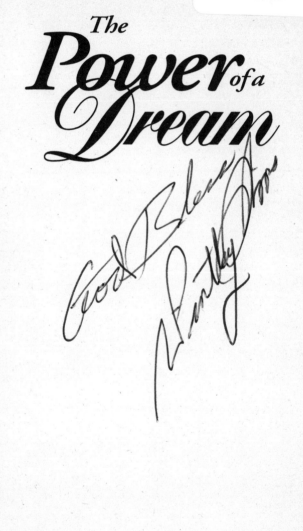

God Bless

The Power of a Dream

The Inspiring Story of a Young Man's Audacious Faith

Wintley Phipps

with Goldie Down

ZondervanPublishingHouse

Grand Rapids, Michigan

A Division of HarperCollinsPublishers

The Power of a Dream
Copyright © 1994 by Wintley Phipps

Requests for information should be addressed to:

📖 ZondervanPublishingHouse
Grand Rapids, Michigan 49530

Library of Congress Cataloging-in-Publication Data

Phipps, Wintley.
    The power of a dream : the inspiring story of a young man's audacious
faith / Wintley Phipps, with Goldie Down.
        p.   cm.
    ISBN 0-310-20662-6
    1. Phipps, Wintley. 2. Gospel musicians—United States—Biography.
I. Down, Goldie M.   II. Title.
ML420.P496A3   1994
782.25'4'092—dc20
   [B]   94–18294
                                           CIP
                                         MN

Langston Hughes' poem "Harlem" is from the collection *The Panther and the
Lash*, © 1951 by Langston Hughes, published by Alfred A. Knopf, Inc., and
used by permission.

Edited by Linda Vanderzalm
Cover design by John M. Lucas

Printed in the United States of America

  96 97 98 99 00 01 02/❖DH/ 10 9 8 7 6 5 4 3

Contents

Part III

Lord, You Are My Music

Part IV

Dreams Come True

Introduction

It was 1980, and I was standing next to Dr. Billy Graham in the waiting line at the Washington, D.C., Hilton. I had been invited to sing at a presidential prayer breakfast, and despite an outward appearance of calm, I was excited about meeting the president of the United States.

When at last the bodyguards stood aside and President Reagan walked through the door, I was taken aback by his stature. He was not nearly as tall as I had imagined. But his personality made up for my momentary disappointment at his height. President Reagan possessed a magnetic personality, an inner humility that expressed itself in a warm, infectious smile. He had a disarming vulnerability that I found totally captivating.

My wife, Linda, and I, along with Billy Graham and others, were seated at the presidential table. I looked around the huge hall where several thousand invited guests sat at tables set with crystal goblets and gleaming silver and decorated with floral arrangements worth a small fortune.

I realized then that the dreams of a little boy in Trinidad several decades ago were coming true.

Linda and I had plenty of opportunity to observe one of the most important couples in the world. First Lady Nancy Reagan appeared cordial and controlled, less outgoing than her husband, who leaned across the table several times to smile and wink at Linda in a friendly way.

That was also my first opportunity to meet Vice-President Bush. As we greeted each other, I had the strange feeling that perhaps I was speaking with the next president of the United States.

All this excitement took its toll on me. When it came time for me to sing, I forgot some of the words to the song and had to ad lib. Miraculously I finished the song with no major gaffs, and I'm sure that even Senator Lawton Chiles, who had personally requested that I sing "The King is Coming," was not aware of the mistakes. When the president stood to applaud, I felt thankful that at least he didn't know the song well enough to realize that I had messed up some of the words.

When, at the conclusion of the breakfast, the president and Mrs. Reagan shook hands with Linda and me, I gave them a copy of my album *I Choose You Again*. I also gave one to Vice-President and Mrs. Bush. A few days later I received a personal note: "You were superb. George Bush."

I could never have orchestrated that meeting with the president and vice-president. It was the result of God fulfilling dreams he planted in my heart when I was only a young boy. He was showing me again that he would fulfill those dreams in ways I could never have imagined.

How does a child, confused and destined for failure, reach a place of fulfillment and contentment? How does a poor child from Trinidad get opportunities to sing for three American presidents as well as the presidents and government officials of Angola, Congo, Fiji, Mozambique, South Africa, and Zambia?

Only God knows how dreams become reality. But most of us underestimate the power in our dreams. To dream is an audacious act of faith. It is the ability to endow the heart with the gift of vision. It is believing in the substance of things we can only hope for, the evidence of things we cannot see.

Dare to dream. Help your children dream. Reach out and take the dream God has for you.

POWER OF A DREAM

I was born down by the railroad tracks,
No fancy clothes to put on my back,
Couldn't imagine what I was going to be.
I just couldn't see it.

But my Mamma told me, "Boy, there's a God of love.
He's watching over you; keep your eyes above.
You will see all that he's planned for you.
I know that vision will see you through."

That's the power of a dream.
Can you feel it? Can you feel it?
So much power in your dream.
Can you feel it? Can you feel it?

You've been searching for what you're going to be,
Just a vision of your destiny.
I know it's going to turn your whole life around
and you'll be glad you've found

He's going to guide you, make everything so clear.
And where you want to go, faith will take you there.
He'll light a fire way down in your soul.
Take your dreams and touch the world.

That's the power of a dream
Can you feel it? Can you feel it?

So much power in your dream.
Can you feel it? Can you feel it?

If you can believe, you will achieve
Everything you're hoping for.
No matter how far, follow your star.
It's gonna lead you home.

You can feel it, children.

That's the power of a dream.
Can you feel it? Can you feel it?
So much power in your dream.
Can you feel it? Can you feel it?

Part I

A Dream Takes Shape

Chapter 1

Childhood Dreamer

The traffic lights changed from red to green. With a challeng-
ing roar and a thunderous burst of speed, the sleek red Chevrolet surged forward. Like an eager racehorse when the barrier is
lifted, it outstripped all rivals waiting impatiently at the inter-
section.

One by one the other cars fell farther and farther behind.
Only the silver blur of a powerful Lincoln presented any threat
to the speeding red streak that hurtled down the highway. Soon
the Lincoln faded into the background, and the Chevrolet's driver grinned triumphantly.

The endless highway stretched ahead, black and empty as
the throbbing motor ate up the miles and the driver's small
hands tightened on the steering wheel. A wide, triumphant
smile curved his lips, and his dark eyes gleamed with delight.
No automobile on the road could keep up with his, and no driver was as good as he was, maybe not in the whole world. His
smile became a low, exultant chuckle.

For a long time the two raced on, human and machine
welded in an unbeatable duet, a whirring, daring dynamo. They

raced to an appointment with destiny. With terrifying sudden-
ness a warning sign loomed ahead. The driver desperately
pumped the brakes. His body leaned sideways as the huge car
banked around the steep bend, its tires skidding frantically on
the stony shoulder. For a moment he felt panic as he wildly
struggled to maintain control. Then he moved on again, dashing madly along the blacktop.

Snatching a quick glance in the rearview mirror, the driver saw a distant vehicle gaining ground, steadily catching up
with his red Chevrolet. The driver's eyes narrowed. He gripped
the steering wheel, determined not to yield his crown without
a struggle. His bare foot reached for the gas pedal. Almost mes-
merized, he watched the speedometer's quivering needle climb
to eighty . . . ninety . . . one hundred miles an hour. How fast
did he dare to go and still hold this mechanical monster on a
straight course?

Suddenly a voice broke in, drowning the motor's rhythmic hum. "Wintley! It's time for supper. You'd better come in
now."

As fast as if someone had pushed a stop button, the bare-
foot five-year-old let go of the steering wheel. The driver and
the shiny red Chevrolet vanished like a burst bubble, and in
their place stood a battered red tricycle and a small, curly-
haired boy.

I've always been a dreamer. As far back as my memory
takes me, I recall dreaming, not night dreams, the kind that
result from eating too many spiced roti and too much watermelon, but daydreams, the kind of dreams one dreams when
reality becomes unbearable.

I was born in 1955, in San Fernando, Trinidad, an island
in the West Indies, just north of the continent of South America. My mother says that I, her firstborn, was a contented yet
adventuresome baby, willing to amuse myself for hours on end.

Which was just as well for her, I suppose, because I was only fifteen months old when my brother, Wendell, was born. I don't remember any of that, of course, but I can imagine how busy she was, raising us alone for much of the first ten years of my life.

I must have been four or five years old when I slowly became aware that my tall, handsome father, Oxley Phipps, earned a living by doing carpentry. He could drive a nail faster than anyone living, so I thought, and he could saw lumber so straight you could sketch a blueprint by it.

My mother and father were special people, clever, witty, strong-willed, loving, sociable. They got along well with everyone except each other. Even as a small child, I sensed that something was wrong. I would wake up sometimes at night and hear their voices. Sometimes I would see my mother crying.

I got to be like a weather reporter. I could tell when a storm was brewing. The steadily rising inflection of their voices warned me of what was imminent. In my mind I would run out to the backyard of wherever we were living and grab my tricycle. That battered old three-wheeler, dented and scratched and rusted in places, was my magic carpet.

I would ride around to the front of the house and haul the tricycle onto the ledge overlooking the street. After turning the trike onto its side, I would use the back side wheel as a steering wheel. Sometimes my imaginary vehicle was a Lincoln or Cadillac or other fancy American car. Sometimes it was a giant transport truck, hauling contraband from place to place.

At other times my red tricycle became an airplane soaring high above the clouds, carrying me far away from Trinidad to new places, with new adventures. I imagined myself wearing a leather helmet, gloves, and thick-lensed goggles as I peered at the instrument panel and directed my open-cockpit plane up, up into the azure sky. Sometimes I preferred to wear a silver-buttoned uniform and sit at the controls of a huge metal monster that rose heavily into the air and roared off into space.

My aunt Adina must have heard me say that I wanted to be a pilot when I grew up because she gave me a book about planes and flying. As I pored over its pages, studying the pictures and diagrams, I dreamed of flying high above the earth, above the petty annoyances of life, above my social state, carried away to some far-off place where everything was perfect.

In my daydreams I soared high above all the unpleasant memories I wanted to leave behind. Flying meant escape from the surly bonds of earth and reaching up for a glorious place of peace and freedom.

I have few memories of a normal family life. Periodically my parents lived together, and for that short time we were a real family, living in a house as other families do. Dad went off to his carpentry work, Mother to her teaching job, and Wendell and I to school. Weekends we attended church, spent time at the beach, or visited relatives. But all too soon the raised voices and angry accusations began again. And when life became unbearable, I retreated into my dream world. It was so much more pleasant than my real world.

To a child, dreams are more than just animated flights of fancy. They are part hope, part illusion, part pretense, and part prayer. Dreams carry children soaring high above the anguish of their circumstance into a galaxy where anything is possible. Dreams take children to a hallowed place, where all that is conceived can be achieved and where all that is envisioned can be accomplished.

Dreams carry within them hope and healing. The ability to dream is one of the most mysterious and glorious privileges of the human heart. From the time I was a young child, I somehow understood that dreaming was a gift from God. Before I knew God personally, my dreams were my only link to him.

My dreams became for me my lifeline. That's why to know me, you must know my dreams. To understand me, you must understand something of their place and power in my life.

Those who dream by day are cognizant of many things
which escape those who dream by night.

Edgar Allen Poe
Eleonora

♪

Chapter 2

Unfulfilled Dream

Except for my dreams, I remember few outstanding things about my early childhood. Weekdays I attended school, and on weekends I went to church. My mother took her Christian faith seriously, but my father at that time wasn't active in any church.

Our family wasn't rich, but we weren't bone poor either. I've never been really hungry, and I've never gone without shoes. Mother, with help from Dad, kept us neatly dressed, particularly for school. On weekends we wore short gray trousers and pink terylene shirts. I well remember when terylene, an early form of polyester, reached our island. Terylene was the new wonder fabric guaranteed to stand up to lots of wear and tear. My brother, Wendell, and I surely gave it a workout.

I don't recall what we were wearing the day Mom decided to take us on a visit to relatives in Tobago, another island off the north coast of Trinidad. Going to Tobago meant an overnight trip on an inter-island steamer, and Wendell and I were as excited as two kittens in a basketful of yarn. Wendell was four then, so I must have been nearing six years old.

Like most other Trinidadians, our family loved the sea. Because Trinidad is small, about fifty miles long and forty miles wide, we had frequent contact with the sea.

Mother took us to the shore, where we paddled and played, reveling in the soft swishing sound of sea on sand and the feel of cool waves swirling about our legs. While Mom and Wendell would build sandcastles, I would stand in the surf and gaze far out to where the blue sea and the blue sky met in a long straight line that Mom said was called the horizon.

I would shade my eyes with my hand and wonder what lay beyond the horizon. I stared into the hazy blue distance until my eyes ached from the glare of sun on sea.

"What's out there behind the horizon?" I asked once. Mom's answer didn't satisfy me, and I retreated into my dreams. Someday I would sail away, far away from my island home. I would find out what was beyond the blue horizon.

Dad often took us down to the Port of Spain or San Fernando harbors to watch the ships sail in and out. All types of craft shuttled back and forth among the wharves, and Dad took great pains pointing out the different kinds to us.

"Those long, low boats carry loads of asphalt from La Brea Pitch Lake, and those other big ships over there are cargo ships. They bring us goods from other countries, and they carry goods, mostly sugar, from here to other countries. See, they look a bit like passenger ships, but they don't have nearly as many portholes or lifeboats."

Patiently Dad pointed out the differences between inter-island vessels and ocean-going passenger liners, oil tankers and tramp steamers, fishing trawlers and ships laden with exports and imports. We were accustomed to seeing cargo ships steaming in and out, and we never tired of watching the huge cranes loading and unloading the ships while the wharf laborers scurried around like ants, lifting and pushing and yelling directions to each other.

Now Wendell, Mother, and I were going to travel on one of those ships, a real ship, an inter-island steamer, not a row-boat that chugged fussily alongside the wharves or a motorboat that darted like a water spider in and out among the bigger boats. As we walked toward the wharf in Port-of-Spain, the island's capital, Wendell and I plied Mom with questions. How long would the ship take to get to Tobago? Where would we sleep? Who drove the ship? Did it sail all through the night? How did sailors know which direction to go when it was dark? What was a compass? How many friends would we meet in Tobago? Were they our size? Did they play football or cricket?

Wendell kept up a never-ending flow of chatter. I soon heard all the answers I needed and retreated into my daydream world. This new adventure gave me plenty to dream about, and as we neared the wharf, I quietly planned my own adventures.

At the wharf we joined other passengers waiting to board the smart white ship with the name Scarlet Ibis in large red letters on its sides. For a while I joined Wendell in speculating which round porthole would be our cabin, but soon I tired of that and fell silent.

By the time we helped Mother lug our baggage up the gangplank, I had laid my plans. As soon as everyone else on board was asleep, I would go up on the deck. I wanted to look over the rail and see the moon and stars reflected on the rest-less waves. I wanted to watch the horizon as we moved through the night, hoping that I could catch some glimpse of what lay beyond it.

The captain directed Mother where to go, and we negoti-ated a maze of narrow corridors and deposited our luggage in our cabin. By the time Mother had opened our bags and taken out the few things we would need for the night, the ship was underway.

We heard the loud metallic dragging of the anchor chain and felt the vibrations of the great engine turning the propeller.

Then the ship tilted to one side. Wendell's face paled, and he clung to the end of a bunk. The ship straightened and then tilted slightly to the other side.

"It's all right, Baby," Mother comforted him. "That's the way ships are. They roll like that as they push their way through the water. You'll soon get used to it." She was right. She took us up on deck, and we soon got our sea legs, swaying our bodies slightly and adapting easily to the roll of the ship as it steamed into the mighty ocean.

Sometimes the ship hit a large wave, and we lost our balance. On one occasion Mother lurched forward and rammed into a couple of sailors who were looping up some rope. "Careful, ma'am," one of them grinned at her.

Mom grinned back. Her brown eyes danced, and her pearly teeth flashed in a wide, apologetic smile. "I'm so sorry," she said in her musical voice. "You can easily see that I'm a landluvva."

As soon as she had exchanged a few more pleasantries with the sailors, I blurted out, "What's a landluvva?"

"It's a term that means you haven't been to sea before," she explained. "You're a land lover, see?"

We continued on our way around the deck, and before night fell, Wendell and I had explored most parts of the ship with Mother firmly holding onto our hands. "No way are you wandering around these decks alone," she told us when we tried to squirm free. "A big wave might come up over the rail, and you would be washed overboard."

We were suitably subdued. It didn't register with us that such a happening would have verged on the miraculous.

Mother also wouldn't let us climb up and down the narrow steel stairs that she said were called the companionway. "See how steep they are," she said. "Miss one step and you would tumble to the bottom and split your head open like a ripe watermelon."

"No, we wouldn't," Wendell protested, but Mom's word was law.

I didn't say anything. I had my own plans. I determined to climb up and down those very steel steps as soon as everyone was asleep.

Our cabin was so small it seemed more like a closet. Two narrow bunks, one above the other, took up one wall, leaving just enough floor space for us to stand between the bunks and the other wall. A shallow cupboard at one end of the cabin and a porthole at the other completed the accommodations. Bathroom facilities were a long way down the narrow passage.

When supper ended, Mom took us back to the cabin to go to bed. "May I sleep in the top bunk?" Wendell was already halfway up the narrow ladder.

"No," Mom shook her head. "You might fall out. You boys had better sleep head to toe in the lower bunk. I'll sleep in the top."

That suited my plans. It would be easier for me to get out of the lower bunk. I made no protest when Mom hustled us off to the bathroom and then into our pajamas. She heard our prayers and tucked us in.

"Goodnight, sleep tight," she said. "I'm going to bed now too. I feel tired."

In spite of all my great intentions, I guess I must have gone to sleep as soon as my head hit the pillow. Next time I opened my eyes, everything was dark. For a while I lay, still wondering where I was. Then I felt the rocking motion and remembered that I was on a ship and that I had planned a great adventure. I was going up on deck to see the moon shining on the water.

I heard Wendell's heavy breathing, and when I moved my legs slightly, I felt his feet warm against my knees. But what about Mother? Was she asleep?

I lay quietly in the dark, straining my ears for some sound. Soon I heard an unmistakable creak as Mother turned over in the top bunk and a hollow thud as she bumped some part of her body against the cabin wall.

I waited a while, then I carefully eased myself out of bed, wincing as my feet touched the cold, metallic floor. I tiptoed to the door and felt for the handle. It was higher than the handles on normal house doors, and I could scarcely reach it.

Carefully I turned the handle and tugged at the door. It didn't move. I turned the handle the opposite way. Still the door did not open. I tried again, this time pushing the door outward instead of pulling it toward me.

For what seemed like an hour I stood in the dim cabin, battling with that door handle, grimly turning it this way and that and pushing and pulling at that obstinate door. No matter how hard I tried, the door refused to budge. There was no way I could get out of that cabin.

Almost sobbing with frustration, I crept back into my bunk. Now I wouldn't get to see the moonlight like a silvery trail across the waves. I wouldn't get to see what lay beyond the horizon. With the bitter taste of disappointment in my mouth, I fell asleep.

Looking back now, I think that angel hands probably held that door closed. I shudder to think what might have happened to a small boy wandering around a big ship alone at night or climbing up the deck railings to see the moon's reflection on the water.

Not all the dreams and aspirations we have are from the Lord. That is why God allows some of our dreams to fade and die unfulfilled. Sometimes God says yes to our dreams. Sometimes he says no. Sometimes he says wait. Whatever he says, he knows what is best.

Whether or not our dreams are fulfilled, we can be confident that God works out all things for good (Rom. 8:28). God knows that some of our dreams would bring us to ruin. In his wisdom God fashions our lives like a quilt from remnants of dreams realized and dreams unfulfilled.

When you can't seem to open the door to your dreams, remember that God knows what he is doing. Trust him.

What happens to a dream deferred?
Does it dry up
like a raisin in the sun?
Or fester like a sore
And then run?
Does it stink like rotten meat?
Or crust and sugar over like a syrupy sweet?

Maybe it just sags
like a heavy load.

Or does it explode?

Langston Hughes
"Harlem"

♪

Chapter 3

Rescued for a Purpose

Some weekends our family traveled to my grandmother's home at La Brea, a town famous for the La Brea Pitch Lake. The lake spread over the countryside like a two-mile-wide black platter, with acres and acres of sticky black pitch welling up from the ground.

When Mom took us to La Brea Pitch Lake, she explained that the lake had provided asphalt for highways in Trinidad as well as many other countries. We liked to walk down and watch the men and machines at work, clawing out great dribbling chunks of the black stuff and loading it into containers ready for export.

Mom pointed out to us that the road leading from La Brea Pitch Lake to the port of La Brea was constructed on top of the asphalt, and each year the road moved slowly seaward, like a giant glacier. The houses built too close to the lake were also dragged closer and closer to its sludge. A strange odor hung over the lake and surrounding area. It seeped into the houses and permeated the walls, draperies, and furniture.

During the rainy season, the ground becomes so saturated that it can't absorb any more moisture. The water lies around in puddles. This is especially true on the La Brea Pitch Lake because the sticky asphalt has a film that the rain can't penetrate.

One weekend Wendell and I, along with Claudette, my Trinidadian foster sister, who was living with our family at the time, wanted to play on Pitch Lake. We sent Wendell inside to ask permission. We always arranged for Wendell to make requests when we thought the answer might be no. He was the baby, and he could get away with things that Claudette and I couldn't.

While Wendell went inside to make his request, Claudette waited outside in the yard with me. We had already been to church that morning, and Claudette still had on her frilly pink dress and new white shoes.

Mom came to the door and called Claudette and me. She was holding Wendell's hand and smiling. She knew very well that we had initiated the request. "Yes, you may go," she said, "but stay together and don't do anything silly. Make sure that you're back home before dark."

"Yes, Mom," we chorused.

We walked sedately until we were out of sight of the house, and then Wendell said, "Come on, I'll race you down the hill." We were off like a shot, making far more noise than children who had just promised not to do anything silly should have been making. Soon we reached the vast expanse of tarry asphalt and began walking around the edges. We were afraid to go near the middle because we had heard stories that the asphalt there was like quicksand.

Unlike the surface of a normal lake, the surface of Pitch Lake bulged with asphalt masses that looked like giant pimples. The spaces in between these bulges were like channels that filled up with water in the rainy season.

The sight of those pools of rainwater really tempted me. I took off my shoes and began sloshing along the channels. The tepid water felt cool to my hot feet, and I splashed along, thoroughly absorbed in my forbidden pleasure.

As I turned my head to shout to Wendell and Claudette, who lagged a bit behind, I suddenly plunged into a chasm. Water closed over my head. I had no time to scream, no time to call for help. I thrashed around wildly, trying to catch hold of something, anything, but I felt nothing but engulfing tar and water.

I couldn't see. I couldn't breathe. I couldn't scream for help. I felt sure I was going to drown.

Young as I was, I knew that I was about to die and that would be the end of all my dreams, the end of everything that I wanted to do and be. Bright lights flashed on and off in my eyeballs; my brain churned. Madly I fought the frightening darkness that threatened to engulf my mind.

Just when I had given up all hope, something touched my fingers. A hand! Frantically I grabbed it and held on.

It seemed like hours before that hand dragged me close enough to the edge of the channel so that I could touch bottom and get my head above water.

I gulped great breaths of hot air, acrid air, but nothing had ever smelled sweeter or felt more welcome to my bursting lungs. I blinked the water out of my eyes and saw that the saving hand belonged to Claudette. My precious "sister" had risked her life to save mine. After Claudette helped me out of the waterhole, I sank down beside her on the hot pitch, coughing and spluttering, wet and bedraggled, but alive.

"How did you know I had fallen in?" I managed to ask between coughs.

"When you shouted to us, I looked up just in time to see you disappear. When you didn't show up again, I thought something terrible must have happened. I told Wendell to stay right there, and I ran. At first I couldn't see anything except the dirty swirling water, but then I saw you thrashing around. I yelled to you."

"I didn't hear you."

"Your head was under the water. I tried to grab you, but I couldn't reach you. I stretched out as far as I could, but my foot started slipping, and I nearly fell in too. Then I saw this bit of grass," she pointed to a clump of tall, wiry grass sprouting out of a small crevice in the asphalt. "I clung on to that with one hand, and I just managed to reach you with the other."

Boys are not supposed to cry, but when I realized what she had done to rescue me and how close I had come to dying, I cried hard. What heroism.

Claudette had trusted a puny clump of grass to hold her weight as she had strained her body the extra inches she needed to reach me. As the three of us gazed at the grass, we realized that it looked quite ordinary. But this tuft of grass happened to be growing right where it was needed. This handful of stalks happened to be strong enough to support the weight of two frightened, desperate children.

Young as we were, we realized that God had cared for us.

"You're in an awful mess." Wendell stated the obvious as he looked at us. I was drenched to the skin, and Claudette's lovely pink dress clung wetly to her legs, and one of her new white shoes was missing. We searched as deeply as we dared, but we couldn't find it. As far as I know, her shoe is still there, disintegrating in a rainwater pool on Pitch Lake.

That brush with death was my first experience of what heroism meant. I knew without a doubt that pure, unselfish love had motivated Claudette when she had risked her life to save mine. She had exhibited the kind of love Christ has for each one of us. All Claudette got out of her heroic act was four days in bed with a fever and the fervent gratitude of a little boy.

When Mom found out what had happened, she was upset. "That's the third time I almost lost you," she told me. "Once when you were very young, you fell into a tub of water and nearly drowned. And when you were about three years old, you fell into a pool and were rescued. Wintley, I can only say that God must have a special work for you to do. Don't ever forget it, son. He has rescued you for a purpose."

> *"For I know the plans I have for you," declares the Lord,*
> *"plans to prosper you and not to harm you,*
> *plans to give you hope and a future."*
>
> *Jeremiah 29:11*

♪

Chapter 4

Music in My Blood

Trinidad is a land of flamboyant colors and passionate music, a land where laughter and music prevail. Everyone sings. People sing as they go about their daily work. They sing as they travel from place to place.

Even nature makes music in Trinidad. Waves tirelessly lap the shores, providing a background of deep organ chords. Stirred fronds of palm trees become wind instruments.

In Trinidad the festive trappings of the annual carnival hide the drab realities of poverty. All year long local bands and singers with names like "The Mighty Sparrow" or "Lord Kitchener" pour out their rhythmic melodies in preparation for the carnival, which takes place two days before Ash Wednesday. But for months beforehand, the practicing and preparation steadily increase in tempo, ready to explode in one grand burst of music.

When a thousand drums of steel begin playing together, it seems as if the whole island sways to the rhythm of the beat. Trinidad is the home of Calypso, and at carnival time, people from around the world throng the streets and village squares, dancing, singing, and clapping along with the music. At carnival time the towns and villages wrap themselves in a cloak of festivity. Rainbows of colored streamers flow across narrow alleys. Houses peer out from under decorative masses of greenery and exotic tropical flowers. Red, blue, and yellow paper chains and clusters of bright balloons sway in the gentle breeze. The air is full of perfume that mingles with odors of curry and sweat.

Wendell and I were too young to join in all the carnival festivities, but we became caught up in the general air of excitement. Mother found it hard to get us to bed when lights and music turned night into day and people sang and danced in the streets.

Perhaps it was this environment that spawned my early fascination with music, that sparked my musical dreams. Perhaps the music was already in my blood. Or perhaps, like that rod in the hand of Moses, my musical dreams were a compensating gift from God for my emotional and spiritual needs. My mother's father was a musical legend in La Brea. Although he had taken no music lessons, he could pick up any musical instrument and master it within minutes. It seemed that music oozed from his fingertips.

My mother, Wendell, and I lived in rooms with relatives or in tiny apartments that no one else would rent. But wherever it was, music filled our home. Mother sang and played the piano with fervor and extraordinary talent.

There was music in our little church, where Wendell and I sang in the children's choir. There was music at school, on the radio, in the streets. Wendell and I often got into trouble for loitering on our way home from school to watch the steel-drum players pounding out their unfettered rhythms as they rehearsed for next year's carnival. Their captivating melodies gave background music to my dreams.

Mother's old record player was another ticket to the dream world of music. I would put on a record of classical music and curl up in the old rocker. A few bars of Handel or Bach or Beethoven and I was transported to London. I imagined myself seated regally in a plush theater box, surrounded by elegantly gowned ladies and lords, watching the tail-coated conductor's hands as he skillfully directed his players. I listened, hushed and spellbound by the orchestra's muted chords and crashing crescendos. Then I would put on a record of the Sixteen Singing Men, and immediately I was in America, sharing the patriotic pride of traditional melodies. A record of haunting Viennese waltzes carried me in my imagination to stately European ballrooms with intricately carved furniture and decorated ceilings and walls hung with rich silks and brocades. With closed eyes, I imagined the lighted candles on dozens of glittering chandeliers, reflecting off the polished floors. I saw gentlemen in powdered wigs and satin breeches dancing gracefully with beautiful ladies in crinolines. Oh, what a wonderful world lay in my dreams.

My own sketchy musical education began before I was old enough to attend school. When my father was gone and my mother needed help caring for me, she would leave me at Aunt Rebekah's tiny house near San Fernando. "Will you mind Wintley today?" Mother asked on these occasions. "I have to take Wendell to the doctor, and I can't manage the two of them."

I could scarcely contain my impatience until Mother and Wendell went on their way. Then I would tug at Aunt Rebekah's sleeve and beg, "May I play the music, Aunt Rebekah? Where is it? May I play it?"

"Of course you can, Darlin'." Aunt Rebekah's shapeless figure led the way into her cluttered bedroom as she muttered to herself, "Now, let me see. Where did I put that toy?"

She began rummaging among the things on the floor, where cartons of books elbowed for space with piles of shoes and stacks of yellowing old magazines. An avalanche of clothing flowed from chairs and racks, and the ancient iron bed was completely hidden under piles of striped and floral pillows. There was always a peculiar odor in Aunt Rebekah's house. To me it smelled like a mixture of camphor and old newspapers.

Still talking to herself as she worked, Aunt Rebekah expertly sorted through the mess and soon exclaimed, "Here you are, Sweetie," and placed the toy xylophone with its multi-colored keys in my hand.

I was thrilled with that xylophone. Aunt Rebekah allowed me to tap away at the keys for hours while she plodded heavily around the kitchen, preparing roti dough and spicy curried vegetables for our lunch.

"That's enough now, Wintley." Aunt Rebekah wiped her floury hands on her apron and took the mallet from me. "It's time that you learned to play proper music." With unbelievable patience Aunt Rebekah taught me to tap out simple tunes. She taught me my first musical scales and helped me to understand the relationship between notes and sounds.

As I grew older, my mother's sister Adina gave me piano lessons. She was an accomplished musician and taught me a great deal about music, but I still regard Aunt Rebekah as my musical mentor. I remember how she gently tapped my fingers with a ruler when I played a wrong note and insisted that I get it right.

One of my aunts, I don't remember which one, asked my mother one day, "Why don't you let Wintley enter the radio competitions?" I don't remember much about the competition or the audition for the popular children's radio session conducted by "Aunty Kay." I don't know what I sang or where I sang it. I'm not sure whether or not I won a prize. But I do remember that when I heard my voice coming over the radio, I knew without a doubt that music would play an important role in making my dreams come true.

Music became for me the language through which I sustained my dreams. It has never been my goal to be a singing sensation. Music instead has been the vehicle to take me to my dreams. It has been a splendid companion, bringing joy and comfort and peace to my soul.

> *I simply dream dreams and see visions,*
> *and then I paint around those dreams and visions.*
>
> Raphael

♪

Chapter 5

Moving North

We're going to live in Canada." Mother made the announcement as she dished out our porridge one morning.

"Canada!" Wendell and I exclaimed together.

As a ten-year-old, I had no idea where Canada was or how far away from Trinidad it was, but before I could ask, Wendell spoke up: "Where's Canada?" With the porridge spoon still in her hand, Mother explained that Canada was next door to the United States of America and that like Trinidad, it had once been a British colony.

"Your father has relatives there," she said. "They're doing well, and they say we ought to go there because it's a bigger country than Trinidad. When you boys grow up, you will have more opportunities for work in Canada than you will in Trinidad." What I didn't know then was that Dad had planned to go off to Canada and start the new life by himself first, but Mother insisted that we all go. She had hoped that maybe things would work out better for us over there.

Wendell and I could scarcely wait to tell our school friends that we were moving from Trinidad. We talked of nothing else.

All day long I dreamed of what Canada would be like. I picked up scraps of information from here and there, and in my imagination I already felt the snow and tasted the sweet red apples from apple trees that I imagined grew on every street corner.

When I found out that we were not going by ship but that we would fly, I nearly burst with joyous anticipation. We were going to fly! The little boy whose red tricycle had transported him into many dream worlds was going to fly in a real airplane to a real faraway place into new adventures. One of my dreams was coming true.

I was so excited about our move that when at last the great day dawned, I felt sick with anticipation. Mother had decked Wendell and me out with our first tailored suits, dark gray, with new white shirts, and, believe it or not, English derby hats. We thought we looked just grand.

Our family boarded the plane at Piarco airport, and my heart pounded so loudly that I thought everyone would hear it. I was going to fly, really fly.

The plane was a small, propeller-driven Viscount, similar to today's commuter planes, but I thought it must surely be one of the biggest planes in the whole world. I was too awed to speak as we strapped ourselves into our seats and listened to the attendant's instructions.

Then the plane revved its engines and taxied along the runway faster than I thought any vehicle could ever go. A moment later I felt the slight upward thrust, and I knew we were airborne. I was flying!

Wendell had the window seat because he was smallest, but I could see over his head. I leaned back in my seat and watched the fluffy white clouds float by. Higher, we rose, higher. Soon we were above the clouds. I could scarcely believe it. The sensation didn't feel any different from riding in an automobile.

We stopped in Barbados, Antigua, and Bermuda before we touched down at Dorval airport in Montreal. To me every moment of the journey was pure joy.

"Here, Oxley. Over here." Hordes of waving, shouting friends and relatives waited to greet Dad when we finally cleared customs and picked up our baggage.

Dad introduced us to all of them. "This is my wife, Elaine, and these are my two boys, Wintley and Wendell."

Everyone was happy to see us. Our friends and relatives kissed us and hugged Mom while we eyed our cousins as warily as they eyed us. All around the airport people welcomed families and loved ones. Suddenly I was overcome by the confusion of sound and color.

All the talking and the laughing and the exuberance overwhelmed me, and I drew back and retreated into my dreams. This time they were not such impossible dreams. I sensed, even then, that this new place would be my launching place. Somehow I knew that living in Canada would help make my dreams come true.

It didn't take long for Dad to find a job as a janitor. Wendell and I began school at the Carnation Elementary School. We lived with a succession of relatives until we eventually found a third-floor apartment of our own.

Gradually we settled into our new country. It wasn't easy. Even though we had never heard the term "culture shock," our whole family felt it. Everything was so different from the easygoing life in Trinidad. Here were tall buildings, taller than I had ever imagined, and vehicles of all kinds speeding through the city streets. No matter what time of night I woke up, the roar of traffic sounded as loud as it did at noon.

In this new place people rushed along the sidewalks, pushing and shoving, racing to get wherever they were going. No one ever seemed to stop and pass the time of day with a friend or neighbor. We missed the throbbing sound of drums or people singing and dancing in the alleys.

Nearly everyone was white-skinned, and most of the people spoke French, which we didn't understand. For a while we were homesick and felt as if we didn't belong.

We nearly froze that first winter. We were accustomed to a balmy tropical climate, and Canada's cold seeped right into our bones. Sometimes the temperature was thirty below freezing, and Wendell and I bundled up like Arctic explorers to walk to school. Even then our noses went pale with cold, and we raced along our street from one apartment block to the next, warming ourselves in each heated lobby for a few minutes before dashing out onto the sidewalk and racing to the next haven. Our breath hung in the air like steam from a boiling kettle. We had never experienced anything like it before.

Mother found a church not far away, and we began to find new friends there. Wendell and I sang in the church choir. We both took after Mother in that we loved music. Mother could play the piano like no one else, so lively and happy that she would have everyone else feeling happy.

Sad to say, moving to a different country didn't heal our parents' relationship. We had been in Montreal only about a year and a half when Mother went to live in Toronto, Ontario. She said she was going to get further education so she could teach in Canada. She never returned, and eventually our parents divorced.

Wendell was devastated when Mother left. He cried often. I retreated even further into my dream world. No matter what happened, I could blot it out of my mind. My dreams carried me through dark valleys and over difficult emotional terrain. Sometimes my dreams were like bread to a hungry, lonely heart. Other times my dreams were a hand for me to hold.

In my dreams I could be happy. And I felt a power in my dreams. I felt that someday the happy contentment I felt in my dreams would become reality.

There we were, two young boys and a father, left to get on with life. Dad was a great cook and housekeeper. He changed his work shift and took a janitor job from eleven at night to seven in the morning so that he could look after us. Relatives helped, and as we grew older, Wendell and I helped with chores.

Dad often took us out on weekends, and sometimes we went to the airport to meet arriving relatives and friends. I reveled in these outings. While the others talked and laughed, I watched everything that went on. I saw the porters trundling back and forth. I was particularly fascinated by the carousel going endlessly round and round, with baggage of all shapes and sizes and colors teetering precariously on its moving belt. Battered suitcases with scuffed corners and broken handles told of numerous journeys to faraway places. Shapeless vinyl carryalls belonging to ordinary passengers leaned drunkenly against expensive leather bags embossed with gold monograms of their affluent owners. I strained to read the labels plastered on sides and tied to handles.

"Come along, boys," Dad's voice pierced my consciousness. "Time to go home." As I hurried toward Dad, I snatched a handful of red-and-white luggage tags and stuffed them into my pocket.

When we arrived home, I shut my bedroom door and spread the tags out on my bed. In my best handwriting I printed "Wintley Phipps, flight 393, London." "Wintley Phipps, flight 676, Paris." "Wintley Phipps, flight 283, Zurich."

Deep in my heart I knew that someday I would be writing those luggage tags for real. Our new life in Canada expanded my horizons and gave me another vista from which to view the world. I began to feel that those faraway places that I had only dreamed about were moving closer to my reach.

I found it hard to settle into school. I didn't realize it then, but children of immigrants often feel the way I felt. I didn't know where I belonged. When people heard that I came from Trinidad, they would invariably say, "From Trinidad, eh? Then you must be good at cricket." But I wasn't. I had been too young to learn to play cricket before we left Trinidad. I wasn't a

Trinidadian, but Trinidadian, but some felt I wasn't a Canadian either: I couldn't ski. I later tried to play hockey, but because I didn't skate very well, the coach made me a goalie. I soon realized that playing goalie in hockey is like signing up for a course in physical abuse.

When I felt like a failure in many areas of my life, I fell back on the one thing I did well: sing. A talent scout had heard me sing a popular song and invited me to attend Town of Mount Royal High School, an exclusive school in an affluent Montreal neighborhood. I wasn't sure I wanted to go to the school.

"Go on, Wintley," my dad urged. "You attend school there. It's a great privilege." Dad wasn't one for wearing his heart on his sleeve and making great speeches, but I could see that he was proud that I had the opportunity to attend such a well-known school.

"They won't sing my kind of music," I almost acted sullen about the whole thing. The truth was, I wasn't sure I wanted to attend a school where I would be one brown face among hundreds of white ones.

"I'll stick out like a sore thumb."

"Don't worry about that. It's what's inside that counts," Dad replied. My dad knew then what I would come to know only later in my life: we need to define ourselves from the inside out rather than from the outside in.

It turns out that attending Mount Royal was one of the best things that ever happened to me. My experiences there helped shape my dreams and define my horizons.

Hope deferred makes the heart sick,
but a longing fulfilled is a tree of life.

Proverbs 13:12

♪

Chapter 6

Fallen Heroes and Misguided Dreams

I became a teenager during the sixties, and the sixties' music was my music. The repetitive sounds hypnotized me. I aped my singing idols. I wore gold chains around my neck and decked my fingers with cheap rings. I wore skin-tight jeans and loose flowing shirts or no shirt at all, only a vest, unbuttoned to show my immature, hairless chest. I rotated my shoulders, wiggled my hips, and imitated the affected gait of the popular pop stars. I was a walking identity crisis.

I looked to the heroes of the rock-music world to define who I was and give me a clue as to what I could become. By this time my voice had changed to a manly bass. My relatives and friends plied me with Paul Robeson records and cassettes. Sometimes, when I was alone, I would tuck my chin onto my chest and deepen my voice to sing "Old Man River." I dreamed I was Paul Robeson, the idol of millions.

At other times I jerked and contorted my body like Marvin Gaye. I dreamed of having what the stars of Woodstock and Motown had. I was enamored with the glitter and glamour, the travel, the adulation, the prospect of finding my identity through show business.

I was on my way to school one day when Reggie, my best friend, caught up with me. "Hey, Wintley," he panted. "Guess who's coming to town?" Without waiting for me to ask, he blurted out, "Sly and the Family Stone."

"When?" I demanded. I don't think I had ever felt so excited.

"They'll be at the Forum in a few weeks."

The Forum. I knew the Forum well. It was the biggest indoor stadium in Montreal. I had been there a couple of times to see my other heroes, the Montreal Canadians' hockey team.

The thought of hearing Sly Stone live just about blew my mind. "We've got to see him," I said. "Right after school I'll phone for tickets."

All day I floated around in a daze. Imagine Sly, the father of funky music, the greatest pop music innovator, coming to Montreal. What an opportunity. What luck. I raced home from school, found the Forum number, and dialed.

"I want two tickets for the Family Stone concert, please."

"I'm sorry, sir. The tickets are all sold out."

Sold out! I felt as if someone had punched me in the stomach. It simply couldn't be true.

"Anywhere at all will do," I pleaded. "It doesn't have to be the best seats. I've just got to see that show."

"I'm sorry," the woman repeated. "Every seat is sold out." I heard the click as she broke the connection.

I called Reggie and told him what had happened. "What are we going to do?" I asked. "I've got to get to that concert."

Reggie didn't have any suggestions. For the next few days I stewed over the problem, racking my brains for a solution. What could I do? I had to see Sly. But how?

Obstacles and challenges never deter dreamers. Dreamers understand that desperate situations call for daring solutions.

Eventually I thought of a plan. I figured that if the stars of the television show "Mission Impossible" could bluff their way into foreign countries, surely a little conniving could get us into the Montreal Forum.

Reggie's eyes widened when I told him what I planned to do, but I had to talk hard and fast to persuade him to be in with me on this one. Reggie wanted to hear Sly as much as I did, but I wasn't sure he had as much nerve as I had.

The next day I telephoned the Forum again. When the operator answered, I pitched my voice real low and asked, "Is this the Montreal Forum? I would like to speak to the main supervisor."

"One moment, please," she said, and then I heard this French Quebecois accent say, "Allo, Can I help you?"

"Yes," I replied in my deepest resonant bass. "This is Bill Canton, calling from New York. I'm with the press, and my colleague and I are coming up to cover the Sly Stone concert. I would be most appreciative if you would make special arrangements for us."

"Certainly, Mr. Canton," said the supervisor. "When you arrive, just come through the stage door and ask for me." I couldn't believe my ears. Could we pull it off?

The night of the concert I borrowed a couple of cameras and hung them around my neck. Reggie did the same. We couldn't find any fancy cameras, and as I recall one of them was a Polaroid.

We dressed as unobtrusively as we could, but if I said that Reggie and I managed to look like a couple of reporters, it would be like saying that two penguins resembled finalist puff poodles at a dog show.

We went to the Forum and found our way to the stage door. "The main supervisor, please," I said to the attendant. "Tell him that Mr. Canton from New York is here." My heart was nearly pounding out of my chest, and my knees were trembling. I didn't dare glance at Reggie. I knew he would be feeling more scared than I was.

Within a couple of minutes a stocky French-Canadian man approached us. "Come right this way," he said with a smile. "I'll show you the seats I have reserved for you. How was your trip?"

He led the way through a maze of corridors and locker rooms, and we hurried after him as fast as our shaking legs would allow. As we went along, he kept up a patter of small talk. After showing us our seats, he said, "Now let me show you the dressing rooms I have reserved for you."

Dressing rooms? I couldn't believe it, but there they were. Two dressing rooms close to the dressing rooms that Sly would occupy: one for Reggie and one for me.

With a wave of his hand the supervisor cut short our thanks. "Mr. Canton, I've reserved these two dressing rooms for you and your colleague. Have a wonderful evening."

After the man had gone, Reggie and I stared at each other in disbelief. Was it really true? We didn't say anything out loud in case someone overheard us. We didn't go walking around backstage either; we were afraid that would increase our chances of blowing our cover. The concert began and the opening act started playing.

Sly hadn't arrived yet. We found out which door he was expected to come through, and we took up a position nearby. We waited and we waited. The music increased in volume. The opening singers screeched their way through popular numbers. The capacity crowd clapped and stamped. An hour passed. Another hour dragged by.

My knees had stopped trembling, but I was still nervous, expecting any moment to be found out. Every time anyone walked toward us or even looked in our direction, my heart began to pound. But nothing unusual happened. The band played on and on.

I grew tired of standing near the door, trying to look like a reporter. The crowd in the Forum was becoming restless. We heard hooting and whistling, and people began chanting, "Sly-y. Sly-y. Sly-y."

Then, above the commotion, I detected a backstage buzz, and people began to scurry around. Word spread like a prairie fire: "Sly has arrived."

Reggie and I lifted our cameras. Attendants rushed out to the limousine. Several men exited the vehicle and opened the rear door. I stood shocked as I saw a frail, disoriented heap of a man in his late twenties being lifted out and almost literally carried into his dressing room. My jaw sagged. Was this Sly? I felt betrayed.

Sly's helpers hustled him into the hockey team's shower stall and turned the water on him. Within seconds he was drenched and screaming as if possessed.

"What's the matter?" I asked an attendant standing near me. "Is he all right?"

I didn't think it was possible that Sly could have heard my question above the sound of the water and the men trying to soothe him. Maybe he caught a glimpse of Reggie and me draped in cameras and was afraid of any pictures or reporters around just then. I don't know what triggered it, but suddenly he began screeching at the top of his voice: "Get him out of here. Get him out of here."

One of his helpers came over to us and said politely, "I think you'd better leave."

Reggie and I slunk out, and an usher showed us to the press seats. The audience waited yet longer before Sly revived and got out onto the stage and began his concert. After waiting all those hours, the crowd went wild. The noise nearly lifted the roof off the Forum. I doubt that anyone minded that we could scarcely hear Sly's voice above the pulsating rhythms of "I Want to Take You Higher."

I know I didn't. I just sat there stunned, not really enjoying the show. My brain whirled and flashed like white-hot strobe lights. Was that pitiful creature the famous rock star? Whatever had happened to my hero, the mythical musician who loomed larger than life in my imagination?

It took me some time to recover from the shock of seeing my idol as he really was. That night I lost a hero. I no longer wanted to be like Sly. That night I also lost something else. I lost possession of a dangerous dream. The dream of being a rock star. I came face to face with the fact that certain dreams carry certain consequences.

By 1969, however, I had forgotten the power of my disillusionment with Sly Stone. I had found another hero. He wore a tuxedo, and he sang with unusual power and feeling. His name was Tom Jones, and he took the musical world by storm.

I still thought that show business was the pathway to making my dreams come true, and there was Tom Jones, larger than life. By comparison to Woodstock and the rock scene with which I had identified myself, Tom Jones looked like a choir boy, but a choir boy who was macho and masculine enough to intrigue me.

When Tom Jones gave a concert in Montreal, I didn't have enough money to buy a ticket, but I managed to find out that he was staying at the Four Seasons. I dressed as conservatively as I could and went along to the hotel. No one challenged me. I entered the lobby and hung around, hoping for just a glimpse of the suave Welshman with the golden voice.

As I loitered around, trying to merge into the decor, a group of people entered the lobby. They talked and laughed with each other, looking toward the door every time it opened.

I plucked up my courage and spoke to the man standing nearest me. "Are you waiting for Tom?" I asked.

"Yes," he said. "Are you?"

"Yes."

"Well, come on up to his suite with us. He should be along shortly." The man ushered me into the elevator along with the rest, and soon I was in Tom Jones's hotel suite. I had to pinch myself. I had never before seen anything like this room, with carpet so thick my shoes sunk into it. Heavy velvet drapes and matching sofa cushions. Gold-framed mirrors and pictures on the walls, and flowers, bouquets, and vases of gorgeous blossoms filling every nook and corner of that vast sitting room.

As the conversation flowed back and forth, I began to realize who these people were. The man who had invited me upstairs was Jones's road manager, and the others were friends. There I was, an unknown schoolboy, seated regally in a cushioned armchair just like the rest of them.

"So, you are a singer?" The manager asked.

"I try," I replied modestly.

"Then sing something for us."

My brain whirled at the unexpected request. My mouth opened. "Oh, no," I protested weakly. "I couldn't do that. Not right now. Not here without music."

He nodded but he appeared puzzled that I would refuse the chance of singing for Jones's manager and friends. I was puzzled also. To this day I don't know why I passed up that opportunity.

Minutes later Tom Jones strode into the room. He was smiling, but to me it looked to be a strange, sad smile that turned into a scowl when he saw the flowers. "What are all these flowers doing here? It makes the place smell like a mortuary." He glared at his manager and barked, "Get them out of here."

I sat silent and stunned. He didn't appreciate all the expensive tributes from his fans.

That night another hero fell.

Heroes are important. Heroes inspire and motivate. They fire our imagination and influence our dreams. They compel us to believe in the impossible.

But I was too immature and naïve to know that I needed to choose my heroes carefully. I was following a misguided dream.

> *Poor eyes limit your sight;*
> *poor vision limits your deeds.*

Franklin Field

♪

Chapter 7

Dreams of Show Business

When I was an early adolescent, I spent time in Toronto with my mother. While there, I tried to audition at every radio and television show I could. I soon learned that hundreds of people worked endless hours at the auditioning game, each person convinced that he or she had just the talent the station needed. Despite countless auditions, no one rushed me with a contract, though I did appear on a late-night talk show. I also tried to become a radio announcer-disc jockey, but I was unsuccessful because of my accent.

I soon saw that my singing voice was not going to get me a summer job when school let out, so I had to use my voice some other way. I became a door-to-door salesperson. I sold or *tried* to sell encyclopedias. When that didn't make my fortune, I tried my hand at house-to-house dress selling. I also tried selling soap powder and other household commodities before I belatedly decided that I didn't have what it takes to become a successful salesperson. I can laugh about it now, but it was no laughing matter then. I desperately needed a job and money.

One summer I worked in the mailroom of the Canadian Post Office. Another time I got a job with a freight company, heaving fifty-pound bags of animal feed onto railroad cars. At least these experiences taught me one thing, there is nothing demeaning about any type of work.

While I was still a starstruck teenager, I traveled to New York to visit Claudette, who at that time lived in Brooklyn. I was wildly excited about my little jaunt into America, and I could scarcely eat or sleep for days beforehand. This was another dream come true. While I was in the city, I determined to see the Apollo Theater, which has featured many of the famous black entertainers, like Ella Fitzgerald, Sammy Davis, Jr., James Brown, The Four Tops, and The Supremes.

My excitement gave way to awe as I stepped inside the historic portals. I could scarcely believe that I was actually standing where the rich and famous entertainers had stood. For a few minutes I waited in a secluded corner and watched the people coming and going, wondering whether I would see and recognize some of my musical heroes.

Gradually my nerve overcame my awe, and I slipped through a private door and edged my way backstage. Making myself as inconspicuous as I could, I poked around among the props and explored with my eyes all the rooms and dressing rooms. I bumped into workers as well as stars, but no one questioned me. With so many people rushing around, I guess no one even saw me as an intruder.

I knew that Stevie Wonder was playing at the Apollo that night, and I was determined to find him. As I wandered about, peering through half-open doors, I finally found Stevie Wonder's dressing room. Among the friends, make-up artists, and assistants sat Stevie Wonder. He was all dressed up, ready for the evening performance, and he had a girl sitting on his lap.

As I stood out in the dimly lit passageway and watched the goings on in that brilliantly lit dressing room, I got the impression that Stevie Wonder was not happy. He had reached the top. He could have anything he wanted. But to my adolescent mind, he didn't radiate the exuberance of success that I expected of him. Another idol toppled.

It was around this time that Russell Thomas and I decided to go into show business for ourselves. Russell and I had been hanging around together for quite a while. Russell, who was a bit older than I, came from a musical family. His music-teacher father had been a player in Duke Ellington's orchestra. Russell's sisters and brothers all played some instrument, and Russell himself played drums. I often joined them at their home for a meal and a family jam session. I don't know whether they knew it, but those little tastes of family life, real family life with a father and a mother and sisters and brothers all living happily under the same roof, were nourishment to my famished soul.

Mr. Thomas asked me if I would sing "O Holy Night" at a Christmas program in his family's church. I felt a bit shy about it, but I really couldn't refuse because of his family's kindness to me. I reassured myself that it would not be much different from singing in my own church, and I had done that often enough. After I sang in the church, many people came to me and said how much they had enjoyed my solo. For the first time I realized that singing a spiritual song seemed to have a greater impact on people than singing popular songs. From then on I began to think of my voice as a key to unlock the doors to my dreams.

But again in my immaturity, I lacked judgment. Even though I sensed a difference when I sang spiritual songs, I was too eager to move forward any way I could. So when a man approached me after hearing me sing a solo at a high school concert and asked if I would be interested in singing at a nightclub, I jumped at the opportunity.

When I told Russell about the encounter, he was as excited as I was. With his dad's help, we got a couple of instruments together and went for an audition at the nightclub, The Penthouse Two. As young teenagers, this was our first venture into show business. My stomach churned with excitement. I had never been in this kind of environment before.

The owner of the place listened to our band play and sing and gave us the job. Suddenly we were headlining at The Penthouse Two. We played there a few nights, enjoying the spotlight and the attention from the crowd.

It was while Russell and I sang at the nightclub that I had the fright of my life. It happened as the result of idolizing another rock star. In Montreal I hung around the CFCF television studios, where they taped a music and dance show called Like Young. I was there so often that the crew ignored me.

One day I wandered into the dressing-room area, and when I peeked around one door, I saw a man dressed in a long, white robe covered with sparkling sequins. My eyes strayed up to his pompadour, and instantly I knew who it was: the one and only king of rock and roll, Little Richard himself.

Instead of backing out, I lowered my voice a few registers and impudently spoke in my raspiest basso, "Who is that?"

Little Richard looked up, surprised to hear such a deep voice coming from a lanky fourteen-year-old. "Where did you get that voice?"

"I don't know," I said. I had become used to the change my voice had recently gone through.

We talked for a little while, and then he invited me to hear his performance that night. As I sat there in the audience, I saw one of the most incredible displays of show-business prowess that I had ever seen. Little Richard manipulated the crowd as if he, or they, were possessed. I watched and listened, entranced.

I decided that it was his songs that got people so excited. I was only a fledgling singer and songwriter at the time, so I decided I would borrow some of Little Richard's songs. I added "Lucille" and "Good Golly, Miss Molly" to my repertoire, hoping that they would help me to turn on an audience just as Little Richard did. Then I decided I would try to sound more like Little Richard as well.

The first time I performed his songs at the nightclub where I worked, I changed from singing to screaming, just as Little Richard did. After a couple of songs, I noticed a grainy feeling in my throat, but I kept right on because the audience seemed to be loving it. I was too dizzy with success to think of what I might be doing to my throat.

The next morning when I awoke, I felt as if my throat was full of sand. I tried to speak, but only a raspy, grating noise came out. I tried to sing, but I couldn't hit the notes. I tried harder. That only intensified the gritty feeling in my throat.

All that day I used mouthwashes, salt-water gargles, and honey and lemon juice. I tried every home remedy that kind friends and relatives suggested. Nothing worked.

After experimenting for nearly a week with home remedies, I made an appointment with my doctor, hoping he could prescribe some medicine. After he asked questions and peered down my throat, he sat back in his chair, put his elbows on the desk, and made his pronouncement. "I'm going to be very candid with you. I don't think I can do anything for you. There is no medicine that will help you. You have badly overstrained your throat and voicebox."

"Can't you do anything at all?" I pleaded in a hoarse whisper. "I'm a singer. I've got to get my voice back."

He hesitated for a few minutes, then unenthusiastically suggested, "If you gave your throat a complete rest and didn't try to sing a note or speak a word for a whole week, it may help. I won't promise a cure. But you have nothing to lose."

"I'll try it," I croaked eagerly. "I'll try anything."

"Don't get your hopes up," the doctor warned me. "You might never get your singing voice back."

That week was the longest seven days of my life. I was so afraid of losing my voice forever that I carried out the doctor's advice to the letter. At home I made signs for what I wanted or wrote my requests down on pieces of paper. Wherever I went, I carried a pen and a little notepad with me. If the teacher asked me a question at school, I would walk to the blackboard and write the answer. As the week drew to a close, I could scarcely wait.

Even before I saw the doctor, I gingerly tried out my voice. Joy of joys, I could speak normally! I tried singing, quietly at first and then more loudly. Up and down my voice range I warbled, and my voice sounded stronger than ever before. I felt elated.

I was so thankful to get my voice back that I promised God I would never again try to sing like Little Richard. I vowed that I would sing only songs that helped people spiritually.

I quit my job at The Penthouse Two. I slowly began to admit that maybe show business would not be the path to my dream. But Satan was not finished trying to keep me from the right road.

I know, O Lord, that a man's life is not his own;
it is not for man to direct his steps.

Jeremiah 10:23

♪

Chapter 8

Satan Tries to Snatch the Dream

"Hey, Wintley! Want to do something really different?" Perry gave me a nod and a knowing wink that clearly signaled that whatever the "something" was, it was not good. Perry was not actually a buddy of mine, just one of the other kids in my class at school. We tended to hang around together because we lived in the same part of the city.

"What's going on?" I asked.

"Oh, it's something really different." Another nod and a wink, calculated to arouse my curiosity.

"Be at Joe's place about ten tonight. Okay?"

Perry disappeared into the recess crowd and left me wondering. I guessed there was something mischievous afoot, but what? It wouldn't be smoking. We had already tried that down in the back alley behind Tom's place. Tom's father was a heavy smoker, and it was easy for Tom to snitch a packet of cigarettes. A couple of the kids started smoking like veterans, inhaling deeply and sending the blue smoke curling out of their nostrils. It was easy to see that this was not their first experience with cigarettes. One of the girls tried to do the same thing, and it set

55

her to coughing so badly that she threw up. That was the end of tobacco for her.

Of course I tried it too. I wanted so badly to be accepted in this new homeland that I did almost anything to keep in with the crowd. In my heart I knew that Mother and Dad would not want me to smoke, but I reasoned that I couldn't be tied to Mom's apron strings forever. Smoking was against all the teachings of my church too, but I stifled my conscience about that and put the cigarette to my lips. A few puffs and I knew that this was not for me. The hot smoke burned my throat and lungs and made me panic: I didn't want to risk losing my voice. I didn't even finish one cigarette. My nose and throat felt raw and blistered after only a couple of draws. While I coughed and spluttered, the other kids called me names and laughed at me.

This was one time I didn't care about being in with the crowd. My singing and my dreams meant more to me than their approval. I made a joke of it. "No way," I spluttered in between coughs. "No more smoking for me, Tom."

So I knew Perry's secret rendezvous wouldn't be to experiment with smoking. I ruled out alcohol too. All of us had tasted alcohol by that time; it was one of the first things we had done to prove that we weren't little kids any more. Not that we liked alcohol. But every billboard and magazine advertisement made us feel that anyone who was popular drank beer, wine, or hard liquor. It sure fooled most of us kids into feeling that we were really "with it" when we downed a cold beer on a hot day. I was never drunk in my life. I never did drugs either. I thought it important to have a clear head and be in control of my faculties. Somehow I knew even with all my curiosity that alcohol and drugs would destroy my dreams.

My curiosity that afternoon kept me from concentrating on my algebra, French, and science classes. As soon as the bell rang, I raced out of school.

At home I had to hide my curiosity about what was going to happen tonight and pretend that today was just another day. Dad was up and preparing supper.

After we ate, Wendell and I had to do the dishes. We had the usual argument about whose turn it was to wash and whose turn to wipe and put away. We watched our favorite shows on television, did our homework, and put out our lunches for school the next day.

I acted as if it was just an ordinary evening, but deep inside my curiosity was bubbling almost to boiling point. I kept glancing at the clock and wishing that Dad would get going. He generally left for his job about ten o'clock, and he liked to have us boys in bed or at least getting ready for bed by then.

I was supposed to be at Joe's place by ten. I smothered a sigh. I gave up all hope of getting there on time. I would have to wait until Wendell was asleep. A bit before ten o'clock Dad left the house, but not without delivering the usual admonitions about switching out all lights and not opening the door to strangers and being sure that the television was off, and all the rest of it.

Fortunately for me, Wendell had already closed the door and gone to bed. When I was reasonably sure that Dad would be safely on the bus, I sneaked out the front door and set off in the opposite direction.

I rode my bicycle as fast as I could, but by the time I arrived at Joe's place, it was nearly 10:30. I remember that because just before I reached his house, I saw the time on one of those bright flashing signs that alternately display time and temperature.

Joe opened the door to my knock. "You're late," he accused. "We wanted to start without you, but Perry insisted we had to wait. Come on up." Joe led the way to the stairs and quietly began the climb. I followed, conscious of my heavy breathing. I was still panting from my ride. At every squeak of the rickety stairs, Joe paused as if expecting to be challenged. Finally we made it to the top, and he opened the door that led out onto the flat roof.

In the dim light I saw half a dozen white males and females sitting cross-legged on the cement rooftop, talking in low voices. The circle widened to accommodate Joe and me. No introductions were needed; we all knew each other from school.

"First," said Joe, "we hold the hand of the person next to us, like this, and we all sit still and keep very quiet."

We all held hands, and then Joe explained that we were going to have a séance. One of the females giggled rather nervously. I didn't feel like giggling, but I sure began to feel nervous.

So this is what the mysterious "something" was. A séance. If I had known that, I wouldn't have come. I would have made up some kind of excuse. I may have been at a rebellious stage in my life, but I had gone to church enough to know that if I wanted stay to healthy, I shouldn't go messing around with the Devil.

"Now I want you to concentrate. Concentrate hard," Joe instructed. "We're going to call up the spirit of Louis Armstrong. Close your eyes, keep your hands clasped, and concentrate . . . concentrate . . . concentrate." Joe's voice trailed off, and an eerie silence settled over the group. We all knew that Louis Armstrong had recently died.

The city noises seemed to fade out altogether. Having our eyes closed sharpened our other senses, and I think I could have heard a pin drop onto the concrete. I don't know how long we sat like that, but it seemed like a long time. It became spookier by the minute. My nerves felt taut as guitar strings. I kept my eyes tightly closed to shut out the hazy outlines of the others in the circle and anything else that might appear. The girl's fingers that held my right hand felt cold and twitched slightly as if she also was apprehensive.

Soon I felt something else, a pressure on my abdomen. A gentle pressure that grew firmer as it slowly traveled up my body, my chest, and my throat.

I wanted to grab at this thing, this something that was creeping slowly upward, constricting my breathing. I wanted to tear at it, thrust it away. But I was powerless. I couldn't move. It wasn't just that my partner on either side held tightly onto my hands; I probably could have torn free from their grasp. But my arms hung limp and powerless. My strength had gone.

At the same time I felt my jaws being forced apart; my mouth was opening. An unseen something was manipulating my mouth and throat. Suddenly I knew that without a doubt a well-known raspy voice was about to speak, and the words forming on my tongue were "Hello Dolly." I couldn't struggle. I couldn't scream. My body was held in a vise-like power. My jaw was rigid, held by an unseen force. But in my mind I cried out, "God save me. Jesus, help me. I'll never attend a séance again"

Instantly my jaw relaxed. My taut nerves slackened. The dreadful pressure on my chest vanished. I could breathe properly again. Trembling with relief, I looked around me. We were still sitting cross-legged in a circle, holding hands in the semi-darkness.

For a few more minutes we all sat quietly, then Joe's voice broke the silence. "That's awfully strange," he said. "Something went wrong. Louis Armstrong was here. I sensed his presence. He was about to speak through one of us then suddenly he vanished. I don't know what happened. I don't understand it."

I understood it only too well. But I sat in cowardly silence.

"Oh, well, we'll try again next week," Joe promised. "See you all same time, same place."

"You won't see me," I muttered under my breath.

In a few minutes the spell was entirely broken. We dropped hands and stood up. Normal teenage chatter began to flow. As soon as I could, I mumbled something to Joe about having to get home before my dad found out.

I kept my promise to God. Never again have I had anything to do with spiritism and the occult. Little did I know that right then and there, all of my dreams could have died. I was fooling with the powers of evil, who could easily have taken control of my mind.

That night Satan almost snatched my dream. But the power that is in the name of Jesus rescued my dream from the clutches of demons.

I know that you can do all things;
no plan of yours can be thwarted."

Job 42:2

But blessed is the man who trusts in the Lord,
whose confidence is in him.

Jeremiah 17:7

♪

Part II

I Give You My Life

Chapter 9

The King's Way

During one of my visits to Toronto, where my mother was teaching school, she and I talked about my dreams. Even though I saw her only infrequently, she seemed to understand me well. She called me her "dreamer boy."

Mother firmly believed that God had something special in store for her elder son. She encouraged me and did whatever she could to nurture and nourish my dreams. "Be sure to put firm foundations under your dreams, Wintley," she would say. After my experiences with nightclubs and show-business people, I was beginning to understand what she meant.

While I was in Toronto, my mother arranged for me to sing at her church's dedication. It was a grand occasion, with people attending from all over the world. In the afternoon a red-haired man named James Bingham played a concert to dedicate the new church organ. Later on, when the program was over and people were standing around in groups talking, James Bingham came up to me. "I enjoyed the solo you sang this afternoon," he said with an accent I couldn't quite identify. "You have a good voice."

"Thank you," I answered. This wasn't the first time I had heard this line. People often complimented my singing and then asked me to sing at their church or school or meeting. But this time the response was different.

"My name is Jim Bingham. I'm Australian, but right now I'm head of the music department at Kingsway College in Oshawa, Ontario. During the school break our youth choir is making a two-week singing tour, and we would like to have you join us."

Kingsway College. I had heard of this school, but I knew very little about it. Mom came up just then, and when she heard about the offer, she encouraged me to join the tour.

Traveling with the choir from Kingsway was an eye-opener for me. I had not been with many Christian young people before. I soon realized that they had a hero I had not personally met. They had something that I didn't have, a sense of direction, as if they knew where they were going, who they were going with, and how they would get there.

I was especially aware of two young women who were distinctly different from the young women I knew. I watched them every day, and I listened to their conversation. When some of the other kids griped about the rain, the food, or the places where we were to sing, Bonnie and Carol didn't join in. Instead, they changed the conversation to something positive. They weren't preachy, that would have turned me off, but they seemed to have the real love of Christ shining through their words and actions.

Shortly after the choir tour ended, Jim Bingham phoned me at home in Montreal and urged me to attend Kingsway as a student. I told him no because we couldn't afford it. Bingham phoned again and offered me a scholarship. Even with a scholarship I knew that Dad couldn't afford for me to attend Kingsway. But Jim Bingham wouldn't give up. "You must come to Kingsway," he urged. "Bring all the money you can, and we'll find you part-time work in the woodwork factory. I'm sure you'll make it."

Dad was delighted to see me off to Oshawa. He told me many years later that the scholarship to Kingsway came just in time. He was almost at his wits end trying to raise two rambunctious teenagers who rebelled against his authority.

I arrived at Kingsway with platform shoes and all the hippie gear that I was accustomed to wearing at public school. It didn't go over big at Kingsway, and neither did I.

I was accustomed to being my own boss, and I found the college rules and regulations to be worse than Dad's. Lights had to be out at a certain hour. Meals were more Spartan than what I was used to, and they were served only at certain times in the day. If students didn't get to the cafeteria on time, they went hungry. Students couldn't leave the campus without permission. Males were not allowed to hold hands with females on campus. Things were pretty strict.

I enjoyed the music part, and I could handle the classes, but the rest of it really got under my skin. For three months I tried to fit into Kingsway and failed. Winter was coming on, and the cold was even worse than in Montreal. Every day the rules seemed more irritating. I wasn't getting along socially either. I hadn't yet learned that in the midst of challenges one only gets back what one gives.

Things came to a head one Friday night when I missed supper because I was late. I was short on cash so I couldn't sneak out and buy a hamburger. I was furious. This was it. I had had enough. Of course I blamed the college, not myself.

Fuming, I went to see Dean Culmore, the dean of men. He greeted me quietly, and I got straight to the point. "I can't stand this place any longer," I told him. "I don't fit in here with all these stupid rules and regulations. I'm leaving just as soon as I can get a train back home."

The dean looked at me calmly and asked, "Is that what you really want to do, Wintley?"

"Yes," I spat the word at him. "I don't think I could ever belong at Kingsway. We're not allowed do anything that we want to do. I don't think I could ever reach my destiny from here."

For a moment Dean Culmore didn't say anything. Then he looked me straight in the eye and said, "For once, why don't you do what God wants you to do, Wintley, instead of what you want to do?" His words hit me like a ten-ton truck.

I don't remember what else he said, but as I climbed the dimly lit stairs to my room, my heart strained under a load of conviction. Instinctively I knew that I would never be fulfilled, I would never fit in anywhere, I would never have peace until I yielded my life to God's irresistible will.

I would never be happy until I surrendered my dreams to the dream God had been dreaming for me. There was no other way. If I wanted to see the dawning of my destiny, I had to be willing to follow the uncertain path of faith and surrender.

Why don't you do what God wants you to do? That simple question changed my whole life.

I reached my room and closed the door. I got down on my knees. For the first time in all my sixteen years, I really held a conversation with God.

"Lord," I said, "whatever you want me to do, I'll do it. If you want me to be a garbage man for the rest of my life, I'll be a garbage man. If the only music I'll ever know is singing hymns from the back of a garbage truck, that's fine. But God, you know how much I would like to travel and use my talent for your glory. If that's your will for me, please open the doors in some way and give me a glimpse of what is ahead."

The Lord didn't give me a vision or a dream that night. The next day I went to church. Nothing different happened then either, except that I sang all the hymns with a greater depth of understanding and I listened to the sermon, really listened, as I searched for a message from God.

I entered into all the religious exercises in a way that I had never done before. A chorus that we sang that day brought me a new vision:

> *It only takes a spark to get a fire going,*
> *And soon all those around can warm up to its glowing.*
> *That's how it is with God's love*
> *Once you've experienced it.*
> *You want to sing.*
> *It's fresh like spring;*
> *You want to pass it on.*

That night God lit a fire in my heart, and ever since then I have wanted to pass it on to others.

The next day as I walked toward the furniture factory, hearing bird songs with new appreciation and glowing with my newly found sense of peace and well-being, two men walked up to me.

"Are you Wintley Phipps?"

"Yes," I answered hesitantly. I had never seen them before, and I wondered what they wanted.

"We've been hearing about you," the shorter man said. "We belong to a Canadian group of singing evangelists like the Heritage Singers in the States, and we want you to travel and do singing evangelism with us."

I was astounded, but I knew that God had just given me a glimpse of my future with him.

From that day forward my life has been different. It seemed to me then that God said, "Son, I know about these show-business dreams of yours, and I know how precious they are to you. I know that you want to travel the world and sing. But if you will just give me your dreams, I will let you see the dream that I have for you."

There at Kingsway, when I was sixteen, God allowed me to glimpse the dream he had been dreaming for me. He allowed me to see his way.

The following few weeks were precious. I had never before had such an experience of answered prayer. I basked in the warm glow of God's awesome love and presence. I had finally met my hero, Jesus Christ.

> *Give us clear vision that we may know*
> *where to stand and what to stand for,*
> *because unless we stand for something,*
> *we shall fall for anything.*

Peter Marshall
Mr. Jones, Meet the Master

♪

Chapter 10

Oakwood College

You must come to Oakwood College, Wintley," Jimmy Wilson insisted, enthusiasm shining in his lively dark eyes. "Oakwood is the place for you. I know you'll be happy there." Jimmy Wilson, a friend who had graduated a few years earlier from Kingsway, had come up to Canada to see his fiancée, Paula. Whenever I saw him, he could talk of nothing but Oakwood, an all-black college in Alabama.

I enjoyed my time at Kingsway College. I experienced a few isolated incidents of tension; that's bound to happen in any multi-racial environment, but on the whole everything was fine, and I was sorry to be finishing up at Kingsway. However, Jimmy was very persistent. He finally wore me down, and after much prayer I decided to go to Oakwood.

Getting a visa that enabled me to enter America for study was no big deal, but I had many other problems, not the least of which was money. Because I was a Canadian citizen, I wasn't eligible for any American educational grants and loans. And because I was attending school in the States, I wasn't eligible for any Canadian educational grants or loans either.

After exploring every possibility, I had to act in faith, just as I had done when I entered Kingsway. The only money I had was three hundred dollars that my father had given me. If the Lord wanted me at Oakwood, and I felt sure he did, then he would provide the remainder of my fees.

When I arrived at Oakwood College and went to register, I filled in all the papers and handed over my three hundred dollars. The woman behind the counter looked at me in surprise.

"Is that all the money you have?" she asked.

"Yes," I replied rather sheepishly.

As she recounted the dollar bills, I prayed silently, "Lord strengthen my faith. Surely I haven't driven all the way to Alabama only to be refused admittance because I don't have enough money."

As she finished counting the bills, I looked at her and said, "I'm willing to work."

She ignored my remark. She wadded the notes into a roll and then looked up at me again. "What did you say your name is?"

"Wintley Phipps." I felt as nervous as a four-year-old caught snitching candy.

"Wait a minute," she said and disappeared into a back office. When she reappeared, she had a card in her hand, and she was smiling.

"This is a funny thing," she said. "I thought I remembered the name. I found a ledger card here with your name on it and a credit of $633."

I gasped. This wasn't funny. It was miraculous.

"Can you tell me where this money came from?" I asked incredulously.

"From someone in Munising, Michigan," she replied.

I nodded. While the woman fixed up my registration papers, my mind flew back to a cold winter evening several months earlier when our bus chugged into a small town in

Michigan's northern peninsula. Little did I know that a woman with a great heart lived there.

I was on tour with Jim Bingham's choir, and as we sang that night, a woman in the audience singled me out. Since Munising was too small to have a big hotel, the choir members stayed in private homes. That night Betty Rohac asked if I, the little kid with the big voice, could stay at her family's home.

That was the beginning of a wonderful friendship between two unlikely people: a white Roman Catholic woman and a black Protestant young man. After that first night, Betty often invited me to her home, where her family took the place of the happy, united home that I had never known. When I spent time with them, I felt a warmth and sense of belonging that transcended all boundaries of race and religion.

It was Betty who had sent the money that enabled me to register. I don't remember doing so, but I must have mentioned to these dear friends that I hoped to attend Oakwood College if the Lord provided me with money.

Sometimes I think back and shudder to speculate on what might have happened to me if I had been turned away from Oakwood College that day. How different my life would have been if God had not used a Roman Catholic family to provide for my needs.

With my registration fees taken care of, I began my college career. Just as Jimmy Wilson had predicted, I felt I belonged in Oakwood College. From the moment that I drove onto the campus, it touched my spirit. I knew that I was home.

The president of the college, Dr. Calvin Rock, took a personal interest in me. From the start it was clear that I was going to have financial difficulties, so he arranged for me to work in the mail room of the administration department. But that was not enough to provide for all my needs. On weekends I arranged for a musician to accompany me, and we traveled around to the various churches, presenting musical programs. Most times the churches paid us by taking an offering. Often the offering barely covered our expenses.

Oakwood College was then, and still is, a place of unusual musical talent. Such groups as The Aeolians and Take Six were spawned at Oakwood. My feet had scarcely hit the college floorboards before I was in with the musical groups. With the successes I had experienced in Canada, I wondered whether I could make Oakwood sit up and take notice. I could not have been more wrong. I was the one who sat up and took notice.

The more I performed, the more I felt a growing sense of competition. Although none of us performers would admit it, we kept anxious ears on the applause meter and the "amen" meter. If the audience clapped and whistled and stamped their feet for my performance louder than they did for the other performers, then I knew I was doing pretty well. But if the clapping was merely polite applause, then I knew I had to do better next time.

If I poured out my soul in a sacred song and as the last notes died away, I saw people blowing their noses and heard hearty "amens" coming from every direction, then I knew that I had touched hearts. But if there was no nose blowing and only a few half-hearted "amens," then I shriveled up inside and felt I had failed.

Of course we all knew that we were supposed to sing to praise God and not to please other people, but we were only human after all. Early on all of us used those meters to gauge our success or failure.

The music community had certain unwritten laws. If a person introduced a new song or arrangement and received much praise for it, then no other person could perform that song. Not on Oakwood campus anyway. What we did back in our home churches was a different matter.

Another thing all of us musicians did, though none of us would admit to it, was to search for an edge, a distinctive area of competence that would set us apart from the others. We wanted a personal trademark, a unique identity so that people would say something like: "Oh, Michelle is singing today. What a voice she has. She can hit high C with no effort at all." Or "Duane is doing the special music in church tonight. Wow, has he got a deep voice! Really makes the old spine tingle to listen to him."

I had not been too long at Oakwood when I heard Duane Hamilton sing. He had the smoothest, silkiest, most pleasing bass-baritone voice on campus. When he sang, "I'd Trade a Lifetime for a Day in Paradise," nobody else dared to try it. His voice was superb. He certainly had an edge. When I heard him sing, I felt like a house sparrow in the presence of a nightingale.

Gradually my confidence and my singing improved. I took voice lessons from Mrs. Alma Blackmon. I am convinced that God sent Alma Blackmon into my life when I needed her most. She became more like a surrogate mother than a teacher. One of the most important lessons she ever taught me had nothing to do with notes and scales and breathing.

One day I told her that I had been asked to sing at a small church consisting mainly of a few elderly people. Perhaps she detected from the tone of my voice that I wasn't as excited as I usually was about invitations such as this.

"Wintley," she twisted around on her old-fashioned piano bench until she could face me. "Remember, when you are given an opportunity to shine for the Lord, do your best. One opportunity will lead to another opportunity and still another." I felt my cheeks burn. I needed her kind counsel. Without it I might still be floundering around in a flood of mediocrity, half-heartedly giving only my second-best while I saved my best for the big opportunity that might never come.

As I began to feel more at home at Oakwood, I began to ponder what my edge could be. I wanted something that would set me apart from all the others.

One night I found it. Dr. E. E. Cleveland came to speak at our college. I had heard many people endorse his abilities as a preacher, so I was eager to hear him. I seated myself as near to the front of the gym as possible, and while one of the speakers read Dr. Cleveland's impressive biography, I watched the man. Dr. Cleveland sat with his eyes closed and his chin resting on his hand. His body swayed slightly as if he was in a trance, and his big feet tapped the floor with an unusual cadence. It was the most captivating prespeech ritual I had ever seen.

What's he up to? I wondered. Is he nervous and trying to psyche himself up? Surely not. He must have spoken to much bigger crowds than this. Then why has he closed his eyes, and why is he swaying his body like that?

As soon as Dr. Cleveland spoke his opening sentence, I knew that he had an edge. We had heard powerful speakers before at Oakwood, speakers who rolled like thunder and flashed like lightning, but no rain followed their display.

We got rain from Dr. Cleveland. We were pelted with hard, heavy drops that penetrated our smug, self-satisfaction. Before Dr. Cleveland finished with us, all our self-righteousness had melted away and we saw ourselves as we really were, miserable sinners in need of a Savior.

Never before had I heard such a powerful speaker. I sat awestruck, watching and listening to this preacher. No one moved. No one coughed. The vast auditorium was so quiet that when he was through, we could have heard a mouse squeak.

What gave this man such power to move human hearts?

Suddenly I knew. That pre-sermon ritual of rocking and swaying with closed eyes and tapping feet was Dr. E. E. Cleveland pleading with the Lord for power to present his words effectively. And it worked.

If it worked for him, it would work for me. Right then I decided that would be my edge. From that night forward I adopted Dr. Cleveland's habit of praying before speaking or singing. I learned to agonize and long for the presence of God to be felt in my discourse or song. When someone would introduce me to an audience, I would sit with my chin in my hands, eyes closed and body swaying while I prayed for the Holy Spirit to use me and whatever talent the Lord had given me.

When I stood up to sing, it was as if I could feel a wind at my back. A higher power took charge of my voice.

I feel humbled and grateful for what I learned from Dr. E. E. Cleveland. I learned that in ministry, there is a big difference between trying to be the wind and learning to ride the wind.

That simple lesson modeled by Dr. Cleveland has been a valuable part of making my dreams come true. I was only eighteen and still seeking role models. I thank God that he gave me one in a man who had dedicated his life, his talent, and all that he had to the service of his Lord and master, Jesus Christ.

It was also at Oakwood that Jimmy Wilson and I, with some financial assistance and the blessing of the college president, set ourselves up as Oakwood's Music Missionaries. We studied road maps and plotted a route that would take us across the United States, singing in different cities and in different churches each night. We sent posters and a letter ahead to the churches in these cities so that the members could alert their friends and assure us of a good attendance at our concerts.

For three weeks Jimmy and I drove across America, stopping to give concerts in Memphis, New Orleans, Albuquerque, Bakersfield, Los Angeles, San Francisco, among other cities. This was just the beginning of what would become a pattern for me in the years to come.

Chapter 11

Shared Dreams

All my life, perhaps understandably, I was afflicted by a peculiar urge to secure a relationship with permanence. My father prophesied that I would marry young. When I reached Oakwood College and settled down to study seriously and prepare for my life's work, I knew I had another decision to make. A vital decision. Second in importance to choosing God and discovering what his dream was for me was choosing a life companion. I knew that if I chose the wrong woman, I could ruin my life and my work.

My time at Oakwood College gave me many opportunities to meet young women. Many of them looked desirable. But how could I choose?

I've known young men who have made a checklist of what qualities they wanted their future wife to have.

- Must be a sincere Christian.
- Must be reasonably good looking but not necessarily breathtakingly beautiful.

- Must have a pleasant disposition.
- Must be neat in appearance.
- Must be able to play the piano or sing or do both.
- Must handle money wisely.
- Must contribute financially to the family.
- Must be sensitive and understanding.

Then these young men looked around to find a person who fit all those requirements and set about wooing her. (Not always with success; the woman usually had a checklist of her own!) While I agreed with the qualities on many of their checklists, I felt the whole idea of a checklist was too much like mail-order marriage. I felt that somewhere in the process should be some evidence of God's leading and perhaps old-fashioned love and romance.

I spent much time praying about the problem. I was only eighteen, but I knew that if I spent too much time trying to make up my mind, all the nice young women would be snapped up and I would be left as a crusty old bachelor. That was unthinkable.

Besides, I already had a young woman in mind. I had eye-marked her the first week of my sophomore year on campus. Her name was Linda Galloway. She had a Jesus glow about her, and she looked like a dream.

That was all I knew about her, but it was enough. Then I talked over my feelings with the Lord. I felt so deeply about choosing a life companion that I knew I needed his help. He knew better than I did what kind of woman would be best for me. "Linda looks like a nice woman, Lord," I said to my heavenly Father. "Would she make a good wife for me?"

I didn't expect the Lord to answer me with the immediacy of a thunderclap, so I set about getting to know Linda. My first opportunity came when the faculty put on a "Trip Around the World" night for the students. Various faculty homes provided food and entertainment from a selected country, and buses waited at a designated point to take the students to their chosen destination.

As the appointed time approached, students flocked to the appropriately labeled buses, "Mexican, Italian, Spanish, West Indian" and so forth. I hung around, watching the young women arriving in twos and threes, sometimes with male escorts. To my surprised relief, I saw Linda and a female friend walking toward a bus. Apparently she wasn't dating anyone at that time. With some chattering and giggling, Linda, her friend, and a few others boarded the "Mexican" bus. I quickly boarded the same bus and sat discreetly behind them.

However, a few minutes later I heard Linda's friend say to her, "You know, I'm not really in the mood for tortillas and beans tonight. Why don't we try Chinese?" No sooner said than done. The two of them leaped up and hurried off to the bus marked "Chinese." I followed a few paces behind. Apparently Chinese food was popular among Oakwood students because the bus was packed. The two young women had difficulty in finding seats, and I squeezed in beside a fat guy at the back. Now I was too far away to hear what was said, but before very long I saw Linda and her friend get up and push their way out of the bus. I quickly pushed my way out also.

The two young women walked from bus to bus and eventually climbed aboard the "Soul Food" bus. I was able to find a seat right behind Linda and her friend. Just in case they changed their minds again, I waited until the bus was rolling before I trotted out my ever-so-original line. I leaned up over the back of the seat and said to Linda, "What are two nice young women like you doing out alone on a night like this?"

She smiled and looked at me with a charming blend of friendliness and reserve: "We're not alone. It looks as if you're the one who's alone." Her soft voice captivated me, and that evening marked the beginning of our friendship. I have no idea what we ate or what form of entertainment our hosts provided. I had eyes and ears for only one person: Linda.

I found out that she was enrolled in the first nursing class offered at Oakwood College. Also, the timing was perfect because she had just broken up with another guy, which explained why she happened to be without a male escort that evening.

As time went on and our friendship ripened, I learned a lot more about Linda. Linda was the sixth of nine children. Her grandfather had been a slave in the South in the 1850s. Her father had married and raised a family. When his wife died, he married again, this time to a schoolmate of his daughter's, a young woman exactly one-third his age.

Linda's young mother, capable though she was, found her large family a handful. When kind neighbors offered to look after two-year-old Linda on weekends, the offer was gratefully accepted.

Mr. and Mrs. Forbes took Linda to their hearts. They bought complete outfits of pretty clothes to encourage her to attend church with them. Each weekend she arrived on their doorstep to have her hair shampooed to get ready for church. She slept the night with the neighbors, and they took her with them to church.

For years Linda attended church with the Forbes. She loved the church; it became her life. During this time she too began dreaming of a better life beyond what she had known.

When Linda was twelve, with a friend's, Sis Bellamy's, encouragement, the Forbes paid her fees to junior camp. Two important things happened at that camp: Linda was baptized, and she began to pray for a husband.

During the camp a woman from Honduras, Sis Buckley, spoke at the meetings for the young women and said, "You girls are not too young to think about the type of man you want to marry and the kind of home you plan to have. When I was quite young, I began to ask God to find me a good husband, and he did."

As Linda listened to the woman speaker, that advice caught her attention. She decided that she, too, would pray for a good husband and a happy home. For several years Linda prayed every day that God would choose a suitable husband for her. Then she went off to school. Gradually the stresses of adolescent life took over, and she forgot her prayer.

But God did not forget it.

One day, a few weeks after our initial meeting on the bus, Linda and I happened to pass each other on the way to our respective classes. We were not close enough to speak, but I waited until she glanced in my direction, and then I smiled. She smiled back, but I thought she looked a little startled. It was not until months later that she told me why. When I smiled at her across the flower gardens that morning, a voice had clearly said to her, "That's the man you're going to marry." After we were engaged, when Linda told me these things about herself and her prayers, I became more than ever convinced that she was the one God had chosen for me.

We began dating consistently. We never went out on a date without praying together before we went. We prayed again when we came home. Early in the mornings before classes began, I would whistle outside Linda's dormitory for her to come down into the lobby. We studied the Bible together, ate breakfast, and then separated for our day's classes and duties, knowing that we were fortified by God's blessing and our growing love for each other.

Another evening I remember from those early courtship days was when the college put on a roller-skating evening at the local rink. This was our first real date, and I told Linda truthfully that I had never been roller skating before and that she would have to teach me.

What a delightful experience to have the most beautiful young woman in all the world solicitously holding my hand, even putting a steadying arm around my waist to help me get my balance as we practiced in Beginners' Alley. I was in no great hurry to become a proficient skater.

About halfway through the evening, a men-only skate was announced. As I prepared to go out on the rink with all the other guys, Linda caught my sleeve. The concerned expression in her liquid dark eyes made my heart thump uncontrollably. "Take care, Wintley," she urged. "Some of these guys go really fast."

"I'll be careful," I promised as I edged out onto the floor.

I discovered that roller skating is not that much different from ice skating. I made a tentative loop around the rink, conscious of Linda's eyes on me. When the music increased in tempo, the rhythm sent my blood racing. I swung away from the rails and into the swift-moving stream of skaters. Around and around the rink we flew at ever-increasing speed. Now I really had the feel of wheels instead of runners on my skates, and I whirled toward the less-crowded center of the rink and did a few fancy twirls and figure-eights before the music stopped and I skated up to Linda.

"Oh, Wintley," she said reproachfully in her sweet Southern drawl. "I forgot you came from Canada." But I detected in her eyes a gleam that made my pulse race.

On April 5, 1974, I asked Linda to keep company with me, and we dedicated our relationship to the Lord. We both felt certain that the Lord had chosen us not only for each other but also to work together for him.

Later that year I bought an engagement watch for Linda. We were both young, and I had not yet formally proposed or spoken to her about becoming engaged. I planned the proposal so carefully that I remember every detail of it.

I wanted my proposal to be something Linda would always remember. I guess I was pretty hopeful of her answer because I paid quite a lot of my scarce cash on some red roses, candles, and nonalcoholic wine.

I arranged to use the apartment of some married friends, Faye and Reggie Washington, to pop the question. They were delighted and entered wholeheartedly into the spirit of the occasion. Faye even thought of some things that I had over-looked such as crystal goblets, a vase for the flowers, and a lace cloth on the table.

On the auspicious afternoon I borrowed a car and took Linda for a drive to see the glorious fall colors. Then I suggested we drop by to visit the Washingtons. Faye and Reggie wel-comed us warmly, put some soft music on the cassette player, and then excused themselves and went into their bedroom.

Linda and I sat down in the living room. We could see the table all set with lace cloth and crystal goblets and candles waiting to be lighted. Everything looked just so, as if our friends were expecting visitors.

"Linda," I took her hand and began my speech. "I've been away in Europe for several weeks, and I've had plenty of time to think and pray about us and our future. You'll be graduating in a few months, and then you'll go away somewhere. I might not see you for weeks, maybe months and" I stopped there. I felt the little speech I had so carefully prepared was not going over too well. Linda appeared edgy. She pulled her hand away, pointed to the goblets and candlesticks, and arched her eye-brows. I wasn't sure what she meant, so I began again, "We might not see each other for months and I. . . ."

My talking seemed to upset her more. She kept signaling me with her eyes and mouthing some words. I had no idea what was bothering her, so I quickly came to the point.

"I don't know what your plans are, Linda," I said, "but I would like to give some direction to your life. I would like to ask you to be my wife."

That got her attention all right. She looked stunned. Per-haps I had been a bit too sudden. "What are you talking about?" she demanded. "When? What do you mean?"

I just said, "Excuse me a minute." I went to the kitchen and ran the tap water forcefully. That was the signal to our friends. They waited a few minutes until I walked back to Linda with the bunch of red roses and the little jewelry box. Then they burst out of their bedroom. They hugged us, wished us well and took pictures of me putting the watch around Linda's wrist. Linda laughingly protested that she hadn't yet said yes. We lit the candles, poured the beverage, and drank to each other's health. Then we asked God to bless our engagement and our future plans.

After we left the Washington's apartment Linda explained why she had been so edgy. When she saw the table set out so beautifully, she thought that Faye and Reggie were expecting guests and that we were intruding. She kept trying to tell that we should leave. But when I ignored her and kept on talking, she became only more annoyed. We laughingly forgave each other for the misunderstandings.

I have heard it said that men and women can trace their success or failure in life from the moment they said "I do." If that's the case, from the moment Linda consented to be my wife, there was nowhere for me to go but up.

Linda and I were married in August, 1976. After almost twenty years of marriage, Linda and I have had no regrets. We let God choose each of us for the other, and we know that our marriage was a direct answer to our prayers. Times were hard at first, but together we shared a dream that kept us pressing on.

We dreamed that one day we would have the kind of Christian home we were deprived of in our formative years, a stable home in which we would raise children and nurture them in the ways of the Lord. The Lord later fulfilled our dream by blessing us with three sons: Wintley II, Winston, and Wade. Together the five of us share the blessings of a Christian home.

We study the Bible together, pray together, worship together, share each other's dreams and hopes.

> *I pray also that the eyes of your heart may be enlightened*
> *in order that you may know*
> *the hope to which he has called you,*
> *the riches of his glorious inheritance in the saints.*
>
> *Ephesians 1:18*

♪

Chapter 12

A Reluctant Preacher

While I was at Oakwood College, I enrolled in the theology course, but I never really saw myself as a preacher. Those distant boyhood dreams of stirring multitudes with my words had long ago given way to the more attainable goal of singing to people. During my four years at Oakwood, I preached only once: the required sermon to gain a passing grade in homiletics class.

Then, near the end of my final year, to my great surprise, I was invited to speak at a church in Nashville, Tennessee. I carefully checked over the invitation; I was sure they had made a mistake and had intended for me to sing. No, they were clearly inviting me to speak. I was shocked. I spent a lot of time preparing that sermon. I prayed hard.

Finally I had my sermon all written down. I edited it and then edited it again. I memorized certain vital points that I wanted to emphasize. I made sure that I did everything according to the rules we had learned for sermon making. When I had finished all the editing, I read it again, aloud. I groaned. It didn't sound right to me. "Lord," I said, "I've done the best I know how. You please speak through me. Use me as your mouthpiece. Give me a message to feed your people."

I was no stranger to sitting on a platform. But this time it was different. I occupied the central chair. I was not the soloist; I was the speaker. Somehow I managed to control my hands, but I know my knees shook.

While the elder presented my brief biography, I went through the routine I had copied from Dr. Cleveland. I closed my eyes, stroked my chin, rocked back and forth, and patted my feet as I went through my prespeech ritual.

That day as I spoke, I felt something I had never fully experienced before. I sensed God's presence. As I spoke, I was scarcely aware of what I said. Something supernatural was taking place. The Holy Spirit was directing my words.

As I stepped down from the platform at the conclusion of the sermon, I felt as if God had his arm around my shoulders. I thought I heard him say, "Son, you did just what I wanted you to do."

One would expect that after such an uplifting experience I would be eager to preach at any opportunity. But that was not the case. I had done my best, and God had used me that time. But I wasn't sure that preaching was a talent he had given me to use.

However, I continued to study theology. Linda graduated from Oakwood in 1975 and prepared for the state nursing boards while I finished my final year at Oakwood. After I graduated in 1976, we moved to Berrien Springs, Michigan, where I pursued a theology degree at Andrews University.

Chapter 13

Nightmare

While we were at Andrews, Linda worked as an operating-room nurse, and I continued to sing to earn money for my education. Every few weeks I would do a concert, a recording session, or some other music-related event. After a full morning of classes, I would drive to Benton Harbor, Michigan, the nearest airport, and catch a plane to Chicago. Once I was in Chicago, I could be in any part of the States within a few hours. I used planes as other people use taxis. As soon as the concert or recording session concluded, someone whisked me off to the nearest airport, and I reversed the process, back from wherever I was to Chicago and from there to Benton Harbor and home.

Often as I returned from a trip, I would pray and thank God for allowing me to fulfill so many dreams: I was married to a godly woman; I was enjoying my studies; and I was continuing to sing. But at the end of one return flight, my dreams almost became a nightmare.

Whenever I finished my singing responsibilities, I phoned ahead to let Linda know when I would be home. It didn't matter what hour of the day or night I arrived, either Linda would meet me at the airport, or if she was on duty at the hospital, she would arrange for a friend to pick me up.

As I returned from a recording session in Los Angeles, I walked through the door at the airport in Benton Harbor and looked around for my friend, Craig Dossman, who was to meet me. I saw him and waved. He waved back, but before I took more than a dozen steps in his direction, two officious-looking men accosted me.

"Are you Wintley Phipps?" one asked in an authoritative tone.

"Yes." I smiled, expecting them to say that they had heard me sing somewhere.

But their reaction was far from friendly. They flashed their badges at me, and the spokesman said, "Please come along with us."

Shock hit me like a bolt of lightning. These were policemen. What had I done? I was not conscious of doing any wrong. I was not a United States citizen, but as far as I knew I had never broken a U.S. law. Shock turned to fear. What was wrong?

I was not an illegal immigrant. I was in America for educational purposes, and I knew that all my papers were in order. There was no need for me to feel scared, but I did. The two men led me into a back room at the airport, and then I found out why I was being detained.

"We have information from the Los Angeles police, working along with the FBI, that you have been trafficking drugs into Michigan." The older man looked me straight in the eye as he said this, probably expecting me to change expression and so betray myself.

A flood of relief swept over me. What a preposterous idea. I could soon clear myself of that charge. Though I still felt shocked and shaky, I managed a weak smile and said, "Well, it feels good to know that I am innocent."

"Oh, yeah," said the second man. "Open your briefcase." There were four or five other men in the room, and as I opened my briefcase, another thought struck me, a thought so terrifying that I broke out in a cold sweat. What if someone had planted drugs on me? My thoughts whirled as I tried to remember whether the briefcase had been out of my possession during the flight. No, all the time I was on the plane, the briefcase had been on my knees or on the floor under the seat in front of me. No one could possibly have touched it. During the recording session it was a different matter. There would have been plenty of opportunities then.

I tried to control my fear as I watched the men going through my belongings. They were thorough. They took out every article and shook it. They picked up every sheet of paper and held it up to the light. They rapped the briefcase, measured it, and felt it all over, looking for a false bottom, I suppose. They examined the lock; they took apart my pen.

As I watched their fruitless search, my fears subsided. I breathed more easily. My confidence grew in direct proportion to their embarrassment.

Finally the men put everything back in the briefcase and handed it to me. "I'm sorry, Mr. Phipps," the authoritative one said. "We were misinformed. Sorry we put you to this trouble, but we must be careful, you know."

I nodded. I was in no mood for discussion. I went to look for Craig. As we drove back to Andrews University, I told Craig what had happened. After I reached home, I told Linda about it, and that should have been the end of it. But it wasn't. All night I stewed over the indignity I had suffered, and like many frightened immigrants, I became belatedly incensed.

In the morning I decided to call the authorities and find out why they had picked on me. Was this another case of racial prejudice, or had I done something to arouse their suspicions?

I made a few phone calls and eventually spoke to a man in the police department. "My name is Wintley Phipps," I began. "I am a theology student at Andrews University. At the Benton Harbor airport last night, I was accosted by two men who searched my briefcase and told me that I was under suspicion for trafficking in drugs. Was this some kind of a joke?"

"No," the man said. "That was no joke, Mr. Phipps. We had seven men out there to pick you up, and the county prosecutor was there to charge you."

"But why?" I broke in. "What did I do to arouse suspicion? What made you think that I was implicated in something like that?"

"Well, Mr. Phipps, you've been making a lot of trips to Los Angeles, and when you go, you carry only a briefcase. You're in Los Angeles only a few hours and then you come right back. Anyone who makes frequent flights to the same destination for no apparent reason falls under suspicion. Anyway, you look like one of those guys from Detroit."

I didn't know whether to be flattered or flattened by that last remark, but that was the end of the conversation. I wasn't exactly happy to have been a participant in this little drama, but I was impressed to learn of the thorough surveillance that goes on in the United States.

In spite of the difficulties and frustrations of the moment,
I still have a dream.

Martin Luther King, Jr.

♪

Chapter 14

The Dream Becomes Clear

During the three years that I worked to complete a master of divinity degree at Andrews University, my course work required me to do some public speaking and preaching. Again I felt that all my efforts were feeble and faltering. It seemed that singing, not speaking, was my forte.

But I soon came to realize that our denomination was not big enough to support a full-time evangelist who did nothing but sing; and even if it was, there were better qualified singers than I. So, I became a preacher who could sing or a singer who could preach.

After I received my M.Div., Linda and I were invited to our first pastorate. Oh, what joy. All those long years of study and preparation were behind us, and now we could begin a life of full-time service for the Lord.

Linda was working at the hospital that day and couldn't come with me to see "our" church in Sandy Springs, Maryland. It was love at first sight. When I saw the church, the old song about the church in the wildwood leaped to my mind: here was the "Little Brown Church in the Dale" right before my eyes.

It didn't take us long to settle into our pastorate, and I enjoyed the work immensely. For several years the church grew and flourished and everyone appeared happy. Then discord crept in. There were several strong personalities in the congregation, and they had no inhibitions. If something was not as they thought it should be, they let everybody know. They aired their views and made known their likes and dislikes in a most formidable way.

They didn't worry me too much. Anyone who works with people becomes accustomed to the noise of the dissenters, but what was difficult to handle was the silence of the good, those who knew what was going on and could have spoken up, but didn't.

Linda and I discussed the situation. I had long ago adopted a philosophy that I would not fight to remain in a situation or a place where I felt I was not wanted. Like David of old, when Saul turned against him, I felt that the faces of the congregation were not toward me anymore and that they did not want what I had to offer.

Only a few weeks later I received a call from Dr. Calvin Rock, president of Oakwood College in Alabama. "Wintley," he said, "I believe you're free to accept a position. How would you like to become my assistant?"

That sounded good to me, but I didn't want to make a hasty decision. "Give me time to think about it and talk to Linda," I said. "I'll call you back."

"There's no hurry," he said. Before he hung up, we discussed exactly what the position entailed and what my duties would be and how soon I could expect to start if I took the position.

Linda and I talked it over. We owned a small house and a car. Not only that, but I had always felt that the Lord wanted me to be in the Washington, D.C., area. I telephoned Dr. Rock. "I deeply appreciate your offer," I said. "There's nothing I would like better than to accept, but Linda and I feel that our ministry lies in the Washington area."

"Oh, that's all right." Dr. Rock's reply came through clearly. "You could stay in Washington and be our East-coast assistant to the president. This job will involve traveling, so it doesn't make any difference to us where you choose to live."

This was great news. I lost no time in beginning my work with Oakwood College. I visited constituents, recruited students, attended pastoral conferences, arranged seminars. The college enrollment grew. As well as that, because I was located close to the capital, I was asked to cultivate government relations and represent Dr. Rock at various government educational meetings in Washington.

After three happy years at that position, the college suffered a financial downturn and consolidated its positions. I was invited to move to Alabama and become director of admissions and recruitment at the college.

Linda and I prayed about it, but again we felt we needed to stay in the Washington, D.C., area. "If you refuse this position, you'll be without a job." Linda put into words what I had been thinking. "Your singing engagements don't earn us enough to live on," Linda added, "and we have to keep up with the house payments and the car payments as well as everything else."

"No," I said firmly. "We have always been committed to you being at home with the children. If the Lord wants us to be in Washington, he will provide."

I contacted Dr. Rock and explained that we felt the Lord leading us to stay in Maryland. Many times in the ensuing months we wondered whether we had done the right thing. Our meager savings vanished like snowflakes in a volcano. We couldn't meet the payments on our car. Our bankcard payments fell due, and we couldn't meet them. Our credits dwindled alarmingly. I was tireless in my search for work, but there are not many positions available to theologians with a sideline interest in education and music.

Just when everything appeared darkest and Linda and I were crying out to God for guidance, I was offered a position as assistant to the president of Bowie State College. I didn't hesitate to accept the position. Not only was it a black college, but the work would be similar to the work I had done for Oakwood College. During my three years with Oakwood, I had taken marketing classes at Johns Hopkins University, and I confidently told the president of Bowie College that I could help him market the educational benefits of his college.

Although my dream seemed to waver for a few years, God is faithful. I knew he had blessed me with a Christian education that was to be used to glorify him.

I continued making inquiries about employment opportunities in the Washington area. Eventually a denominational official, Elder Meade C. Van Putten, telephoned me. "Wintley, how would you like to become minister of our church on Capitol Hill?"

Capitol Hill? The name excited me. I could scarcely wait for him to finish speaking. "Give me the address of the church, and I'll let you know as soon as I talk it over with Linda."

Without waiting for anything else, I jumped into my car and sped toward Capitol Hill. In my mind's eye I saw again my first pastorate, and I hoped this church would be another "little brown church in the dale." When I reached the address given, I found no church. I drove on, thinking perhaps I had gotten the number wrong. No church. I drove the full length of the street and saw no sign of a church.

I stopped the car opposite the address I had been given and surveyed the old house that stood on the site. There was no mistaking that it was a house; it could never pass for a church or even a meeting hall. It was a house. But then I saw something that could have been a sign. It was too far away for me to see it properly. I locked the car and walked across the street to the old house. Yes, it was a sign. In faded letters it proclaimed, "Capitol Hill Seventh-day Adventist Church."

With sinking heart I walked up the path and tried the door of the house. It was locked. I walked around the house, peering into any windows that I could reach. It was not possible to see clearly, but there was enough evidence to make me sure that this was indeed a church and not somebody's private home.

That night I told Linda what I had found. When I tried the phone number I had copied from the church's sign, I learned that the church had about eighty members. The church had renovated the house's interior to accommodate a sanctuary and classrooms. The more Linda and I talked the matter over, the more excited we became.

"It's on Capitol Hill," I said. "Not far from the Supreme Court—and the Capitol building."

"Where all the United States laws and legislation are made," Linda interrupted in an awed tone.

"I'm sure this is where God wants me to work," I said and Linda knew I was referring to what I felt was my destiny.

"Well, we couldn't be in a better place," she rejoined.

The first time I preached to the congregation of the Capitol Hill Church, I told them much the same thing. "Do you realize," I asked them, "that your church is only ten blocks away from the nation's capitol? I believe that God has arranged for this church's presence to be right here, where the great battles for religious freedom have been fought and will be refought." Their hearty "amens" nearly shook the building. The congregation was catching my excitement. "This church needs to grow," I said, "and if we grow, we will soon need to move from this house-church. But we must not move out of this area. God has put us here as his witnesses." Again there were "amens" and heads nodding.

For some time this congregation had felt that it had not enjoyed strong spiritual leadership. Now they were being challenged, and they were ready for it. Soon after I took over the pastorate, the church held a business meeting, and again I presented them with a challenge. Only this challenge concerned me personally.

"My fellow church members," I said, "suppose a man saw a beautiful woman who attracted him so much that he fell in love and asked her to marry him. Suppose that she married him, and after their honeymoon, he said to her, 'Now that we are married, Darling, I want you to stop doing all those things that attracted me to you in the first place.'" The church members stared at me, clearly wondering what I was getting at. So I continued.

"I think we are in a similar position. When you agreed to this union between my ministry and the ministry of this church, you were happy. Many of you know about my singing, traveling, and public appearances. Now that we are 'married' at least in ministry, I think it would not be wise for you to say to me, 'Wintley, we are happy about what you have done in your singing ministry, but now that you are our pastor, we want you to stop doing what attracted you to us in the first place.'"

Nobody spoke, but I could see them looking out of the corner of their eyes at Leonard Hodges, who had been one of the leaders of their church for a long time. I quickly sensed that if Leonard Hodges agreed with me, then the members would be on my side.

I breathed a quick prayer and concluded my little speech. "But if you allow me to do whatever God has called me to do, if you allow me to go wherever God calls me to go, I believe that my singing ministry will continue to flourish and the ministry of this church will flourish and grow beyond our wildest dreams."

There was a long silence, so long that I became uneasy. It seemed that everyone was waiting for someone else to speak. Then Leonard Hodges stood up. He was a deep thinker, and I knew that what he said would be a well-deliberated decision.

I don't remember his exact words, but the gist of his pronouncement was that we should try it out. Immediately the tension eased. Most of the members smiled and nodded, "Okay, Pastor, let's go for it." I noticed that a few cautious people reserved judgment and one or two shook their heads dubiously. But when I began to outline some of the innovations I had in mind for the church itself, the skeptics appeared to be won over. Particularly when Leonard Hodges backed my ideas one hundred percent, they became excited and the positive response was as much as any new minister could ask.

"There's one other thing," I said as I continued addressing the church business meeting. "I would like to try using the marketing principles I used to boost the enrollment when I was working for Bowie State and Oakwood College. I'm sure they will work just as successfully for us as we work toward church growth." I'm sure some of the members were dubious about this new-broom pastor who was wanting to make a clean sweep with his new ideas, but they were swept along in the general enthusiasm of the other members.

In the months that followed I was grateful for Leonard Hodges' unflagging support. If it were not for him, there would still be less than one hundred worshipers in the old house-church, and we all would be nursing a strained marriage.

One of the first things we did was to put a box in the foyer of our house-church so that members could drop in their suggestions. We introduced a few innovations in the meetings such as having the members turn to each other and say, "God loves you and so do I." Another idea that was well received was introducing visitors and new members by name. I did this from the pulpit before I began the service, and it made them feel special. Week by week I schooled our members in the principles of quality control. "The most important thing," I told them, "the key to church growth, will be for us to lift the spiritual tone of our worship. Worship is the heartbeat of the church. If the heart is weak, the body will not have vibrant health."

The church members responded enthusiastically, and the little house-church began to grow. Of course we laid much emphasis on music, and our program proved to be a great attraction. Not many months passed before seating became a problem. Our little sanctuary needed elastic walls to accommodate the congregation that pressed in every weekend.

At a board meeting I urged that we look for a new church home. We eventually became interested in a huge church that was only a block away from our house-church. A real estate agent in our church inquired about the church and learned that it was for sale, for more than half a million dollars. She learned that this old Congregational Church had been built in 1910 and that President Taft had spoken at the dedication. The church accommodated seven hundred worshipers, and at its beginning had a holistic ministry. During World War II the basement had been used as a USO center for soldiers; the facility included a three-lane bowling alley, a swimming pool, and a gymnasium.

The more we learned about this old church, the more excited I became. One wintry morning at the conclusion of the service, I said to the members of our house-church, "We have all been praying for a larger church. I think the Lord has found one for us. We have the keys, and right after we dismiss, we will all go over and have a look at the building." A murmur of surprise rippled through the congregation. It was obvious that everyone was eager to see what we had found.

We all marched down the street. From the outside the old church looked reasonably acceptable. It stood in a historic area of Washington, where the law required that the façade be kept in good repair. But inside was a different story. When the key creaked in the rusty lock and we crowded into the huge, cavernous building, there was an audible gasp of dismay. The church was icy cold and smelled of age and neglect. Part of the roof had fallen in. Magnificent stained glass windows were dirty, cracked, and broken.

The small congregation of fifty people could not afford to heat the entire church; instead they had a small stove down in one corner near the front, and they huddled around that for worship. The boiler had long ago rusted from disuse. As soon as some of our members recovered from their shock, they came to me. "Are you sure this is the place? We could never afford to buy this wreck and fix it up too."

"Yes," I said firmly, "this is the place. I am convinced that the Lord wants us to have this church, and he will provide the means."

Another member said, "Pastor, you've got to be joking. We don't need a church so big. We can't afford it."

"We'll fill it," I assured him, "and we'll find a way of buying it. Let's pray about it right now." We all knelt down on that bare, ice-cold floor, and we prayed. I prayed, the elders prayed, and some of the church members prayed that if this was the church God wanted us to have, he would show us the way.

We didn't get any miraculous answer from heaven right then, and we didn't get any huge reduction in price. In this part of Washington, so close to everything that is important, developers are constantly on the lookout for old buildings. They pay high prices for them, then they gut them and turn them into condominiums with underground parking. Just so long as the historic exterior is preserved, the city planners don't seem to care what happens inside.

Our house-church was worth $200,000, but even after much praying and negotiating, we couldn't purchase the old Congregational Church for less than $450,000. Where could we find so much money? We held a business meeting to discuss ways of raising funds. Our house-church members were all hard-working people, but we had no wealthy doctors or lawyers among us. Raising money would have to be done the hard way.

At that time I had recorded four albums, so I took the initiative and set an example of fund raising. I procured smart blue cassette covers and produced what I called a "Signature Edition," four of my albums with my autograph on the front. I packaged hundreds of them and told the members that they could give four cassettes to every person who donated $50 or more to the building fund.

We raised many thousands of dollars in that way. The church members caught the inspiration and worked with a will. God uses ordinary people to do extraordinary things. The restoration of that old Congregational Church turned out to be an incredible challenge, but with God's help it was not an impossibility. We spent more than one million dollars on repairs. We had to replace the entire roof, and that was no ordinary task. The church has a dome-shaped roof, like the Capitol building itself. We hired a Russian contractor to do the job because every copper shingle had to be shaped by hand. Restoring the inside of the dome was almost as much trouble and expense as doing the outside. The first summer that we worshiped in our new church, we shared the building with a jungle-gym of scaffolding. Day after day, high up on the scaffolding, an artisan lay on his back with his tools and sandpaper, renewing, restoring, and repainting every tiny niche of the intricately carved work. It was a mammoth undertaking. Seeing him at work during the week reminded me of Michelangelo painting his unrivaled work in the Sistine Chapel.

Then we had to install a whole new heating system. The boiler for the system was so huge that it had to be brought in by train. We didn't restore the bowling alley, the swimming pool, or the gymnasium. We needed every bit of the basement area for classrooms, community services, and other projects. And we couldn't provide parking spaces. The church owns only six parking spaces, only six to serve a church that often has an attendance of one thousand worshipers. Members have to park in streets and side streets for many blocks around the area.

Our church is a shining example of what God can do through a dedicated congregation, supporting a committed young pastor. Now we have a new problem. Our church is again bulging at the seams, but we have expanded all that we can at our present site. Still I keep dreaming.

On the whole, the marriage of pastor and church has been a good one. I have been able to maintain a singing schedule and be available to preach at our church over eighty percent of the year. God has abundantly blessed us.

A knowledge of the path is no substitute
for putting one foot in front of the other.

M.C. Richards

♪

Part III

Lord, You Are My Music

Lord, you are my music, you are my song
You are my melody, when things go wrong
Lord, you are my music, forever my song.

Wintley Phipps

♪

Chapter 15

Others Nurture The Dream

Once I gave my life and talents to the Lord to use for his purposes, he has been my best agent and manager, arranging contacts, orchestrating opportunities and sending precious people my way to help make my dreams come true.

The Lord sent countless people to nurture my dreams. I could fill a book with those stories alone. But let me tell you about the ways four special people have helped me along the way.

While I was attending Oakwood College, I earned tuition money by doing weekend concerts. Many times I left the college with only my airplane ticket and a dime in my pocket. But I always felt confident that the Lord would provide. And he did, sometimes in unexpected ways.

On one particular weekend the concert started and ended late. One of the concert organizers rushed me to the airport, but we were too late. I had missed my return flight.

After making many inquiries, I found a Southern Airlines connection that would take me through Atlanta into Huntsville, Alabama. Thankful for that good news, I said good-bye to my friend and settled down to wait. The flight from Mississippi to Atlanta was uneventful, but as I checked in at the Southern Airlines counter for my flight on to Huntsville, the clerk noticed that I was not traveling on the airline indicated on my return ticket.

"That's right," I said cheerfully. "My concert ran late, and I missed my flight." She didn't smile back at me. Instead, she turned to her computer and after checking this and that she said, "To travel on this flight, you'll need to pay another fifty-five dollars."

Fifty-five dollars? I didn't have fifty-five dollars. The concert organizers had paid me fifty dollars, and now this woman was insisting that I would have to pay all of that out to get back home. Worse still, I was short five dollars. I had only fifty dollars and one thin dime in my pocket.

One look into her cold blue eyes told me that I had no hope of talking myself out of this situation. No protests or explanations would carry any weight with this businesslike woman. Slowly I reached into my pocket and pulled out my money and placed it on the counter.

"Is that all the money you have?" she asked.

"That's all." It was now almost midnight, and my poor brain was too weary to try to work out a solution for what appeared to be an unsolvable problem. I had attended classes all week, "sung for my supper" all weekend, missed my plane, waited hours for another one, and now when all I wanted was bed and sleep, this situation arose.

The clerk checked her figures again and looked at me. She wrinkled her fair brow in consternation. It seemed as if she was asking herself what she should do. Should she leave me stranded in Atlanta, or should she bend the rules and let this student through without paying the full fare? With downcast eyes I waited and prayed. When I looked at her face again, I saw that her decision was made.

"I am sorry," she said firmly. "I must have the full fare. I can't give you any of the company's money." My heart sank. "But," she continued crisply, "I can give you some of my own money."

She reached under the counter and out of her purse she took a five-dollar bill and put it alongside my money. Then she quickly wrote out a new ticket and handed it and the dime to me. I stood there stunned, speechless with gratitude. When I regained my voice, I asked for her name and address. "I'll repay you when I get back home," I promised.

The next day I bought a copy of *Desire of Ages*, a powerful book about the life of Christ, tucked a five-dollar bill inside it, mailed it to her. Pat Pullen's small act of kindness to me, an unknown student, marked the beginning of a lifelong friendship.

For the next few years I made many connecting flights in Atlanta, and whenever I had time, I looked for Pat Pullen. As our friendship deepened, we learned a lot about each other. I saw her several times a month, and she became like family to me.

Pat shared all the major developments of my life. When I graduated from Oakwood College, she rejoiced at my moment of triumph. When I married Linda, Pat was eager to meet her. When I made my first album, Pat was one of the first to receive a copy. When we traveled her airline soon after our first baby was born, Pat held our baby and admired him as tenderly as if he were her own.

One day as we talked on my way through Atlanta, Pat confided to me that she had Hodgkin's Disease. The next several years were painful for both of us. I watched helplessly as her face became drained of color and drawn with pain, and she lost her hair because of the treatments she was taking. Sometimes when we met, she was despondent, and I tried to cheer her with God's promises. At other times she appeared bright and full of hope.

"We're licking it, Wintley," she said on one of the last occasions we met. I don't know whether she really believed that she would recover, but I went along with her and encouraged her to keep a positive outlook.

The next time I went to the airport, a stranger sat in Pat's usual place. "I think she's in the hospital," he said. He was only a part-time clerk, and he didn't know Pat. I inquired among some of the other clerks and finally found out which hospital Pat was in. I had half an hour to wait until my plane took off, so I hurried to the phone booth and called Pat. She sounded surprised to hear my voice, and as we talked, I could tell she was genuinely glad that I had called. She brought me up to date with her treatments and her struggles against the dread disease, and I assured her that I was praying for her. "Thank you, Wintley," she said.

Some weeks passed before I flew through Atlanta again. Pat was not back at her place. I went to one of the men whom I knew had worked alongside Pat and asked him how she was. He appeared startled. He was a big, burly fellow that looked as if he could handle any situation, but when I asked about Pat, his face paled. For a moment he seemed lost for words. Then he blurted out, "I'm sorry, sir, but Pat died a week ago."

Tears welled up in my eyes; they still do whenever I think of Pat. I am thankful that this woman touched my life and nurtured my dreams. Her love and kindness affirmed me as a young student and validated my worth.

Years ago, Pat's five-dollar gift kept me going and kept my dreams alive. I've repaid the five dollars, but I'll never be able to repay her for her generosity and kindness.

A second person who nurtured my dreams in a rather surprising way is Betty Rohac, my friend from Munising, Michigan. One day Betty called to find out how we were doing. She asked about Linda's work at the hospital, my studies, and our future plans. Just before she hung up, she said: "By the way, how's your album coming on?"

"Album!" I exclaimed. "What album?"

"Your music album, Wintley. What's the hold up?" she asked.

"You must be joking. Albums cost money, big money."

"How much money?" she asked nonchalantly.

I hadn't the slightest idea how much it would cost to produce an album, so I pulled out of the air a figure that to me sounded like a fortune. "About ten thousand dollars, I guess."

"Right. I'll send it," she said and hung up.

I stared at the telephone in dazed disbelief. Ten thousand dollars! How could anyone have so much money? Even more astounding, how could anyone lend such an enormous amount of money without asking for some security or a promissory note?

Betty's generosity nurtured my dreams as nothing else did at the time. I cut my first album, *I Give You My Life*, in 1978.

A third person nurtured my dreams by giving me an opportunity. I met her one day after I had sung at the Baltimore Civic Center. She came up to me and said, "I feel as if I can talk to you. Would you be able to spare a few minutes?" I recognized her as the host of a Baltimore talk show *People Are Talking*.

I invited her to come to our home so that we could talk. When she came, she shared that she was concerned about her future and career. We talked and shared and prayed. One day after we had prayed together, I said to her, "God has impressed me to tell you that he's going to bless you and give you an opportunity to speak to millions of people."

"Do you really think so, Wintley? Do you think God would do that for me?" she asked.

Well, the rest is history. Oprah Winfrey pursued her dream, and she has been blessed beyond what anyone could have expected. Every day, with a microphone in her hand, Oprah is freeing people, millions of people, from the chains of ignorance, bigotry, and fear.

Then one day Oprah Winfrey helped nurture my dream. She called to say that she was doing a show on gospel music and wanted to feature her favorite male and female vocalists and her favorite group. She invited me to be the male vocalist. Her invitation not only honored me but boosted my sense of worth. She believed in my gifts. That kind of contribution is something money could never buy.

When Oprah left WJZ-TV to begin the Oprah Winfrey Show in Chicago, she encouraged the station to give me a one-hour slot to do a weekly live talk show. The two and a half years I did Sunday Live proved to be an incredible training ground for me and has opened up the doors for me to host other programs.

A fourth person nurtured my dreams by making her skills available to me. I met Patricia Barnes at the conclusion of one of my concerts. She said she had heard me sing at the Kennedy Center in Washington, and she invited me to sing at her church. The Lord blessed the program, and afterward the young woman approached me again. "Where will your concert schedule be taking you next?" she said. I pulled out of my pocket a small business card and turned it over. On the back of it, in the tiniest possible print, I had recorded all my appointments for the next couple of months. The young woman's eyes widened in astonishment. "Is that how you keep your schedules?"

"Yes, that's how I do it." I smiled and shrugged a bit apologetically because I could see that she was shocked by my unbusinesslike method. "That's the best way I can do it right now."

"Oh, no," she protested. "You mustn't do it like that. You could easily misplace that small card. You need some help."

I smiled again. I wasn't sure what she was getting at.

She hesitated a minute as if she was making a decision, then she said, "Look, I want to help you in your ministry. Let me handle all your scheduling." I gratefully accepted her offer, and from that time on Pat Barnes has handled all my schedules just as expertly and faithfully as if she were a paid agent. When anyone asks me to appear on a program, I refer the person to Pat. She gets the late-night telephone calls, handles all the correspondence, and does all the negotiating. In addition to giving me her professional skills, Pat has also used her trained voice to join me in a concert occasionally, and she also has become a treasured family friend.

Whether it was five dollars or ten thousand dollars or an invitation to be on a national talk show or giving professional skills, the kindness and generosity these people offered have nurtured my dreams. God bless those whose dream is to nurture the dreams of others. Through sharing, caring, giving, and loving they make the world a better place

There is nothing . . . in the world
so inspiring as the possibilities
that lie locked up
in the head and breast of a young man.

James Garfield

♪

Chapter 16

Sharing
Billy Graham's Dreams

Not only has the Lord sent into my life countless people to nurture my dreams, but he also has sent other dreamers, people with whom I could share dreams. One of those people is Billy Graham.

An unusual set of circumstances led me to become associated with Billy Graham and his evangelistic crusades. One day a flight attendant recognized that one of the passengers in her care was Cliff Barrows, the music director for the crusades. She spoke to him and told him how much she enjoyed the music in the Billy Graham Crusades. During the conversation she asked him whether he had heard of a gospel singer named Wintley Phipps.

"No," he smiled politely.

"I'll get you one of his cassettes," she said and hurried off. When she returned, she handed him a copy of my first album,

I Give You My Life. "I'd like you to listen to this," she said, "and tell me what you think of his voice."

The first I knew about this episode was when Cliff Barrows telephoned me and asked whether I would sing at one of Billy Graham's crusades in Washington D.C.

"Yes," I said. "I'd be honored."

This marked the beginning of a long friendship and association with the Billy Graham evangelistic team and the fulfillment of several more of my dreams. Although the voice of George Beverly Shea, the soloist for the crusades, was still strong and resonant when he was over eighty years old, the long journeys and hardships of the "sawdust trail" were taking their toll on his body.

Looking for someone to take Shea's place for the Russia Crusade, the evangelistic team invited me to accompany them to Moscow. For five days Billy Graham preached to a capacity crowd of fifty thousand people in Moscow's Olympic Stadium.

It was an inspiration just to look out over that vast congregation of former communists who were pressing in to hear the story of Jesus Christ and his salvation. The sermon was translated, of course, and the huge crowd hung on every word. For more than seventy years the Bible, Christianity, and church attendance had been outlawed in the Soviet Union. Two or more generations had grown up not hearing the wonderful gospel story, and now they were soaking it up like a sponge soaks up water.

It was even more inspiring to learn that another twenty or thirty thousand people stood outside the stadium, in the Russian winter, to watch the crusade on wide-screen monitors. They were truly thirsty for the gospel.

Five thousand Russian Christians made up the crusade choir, which sang nightly in Russian. On the last day of the crusade, as I tried to decide what I would sing that night, the Russian choir director approached me and asked, "The choir members wonder if you will sing a song just for them?"

"What do they know?"

"One of their favorite hymns is 'The Old Rugged Cross.'"

"Do they really know that?" I asked.

"Yes. They do," he replied.

"Then, let's sing that together tonight," I suggested.

We rehearsed "The Old Rugged Cross" together, and because they couldn't sing the English words, they oohed and aahed. That night we concluded my musical portion of the meeting by singing the old hymn together. It was one of the most moving musical experiences I have had.

Before the crusade began, I had intended to try to sing some in the Russian language. That resolve lasted until I realized that Russian is the most difficult language I have attempted to sing in. I tried one chorus of "How Great Thou Art" in Russian, but after that I stuck to English, trusting the Holy Spirit to speak to the people even if they couldn't understand the language.

During the crusade, the Russian Orthodox church was concerned that Billy Graham not advance any particular denomination. After the crusade left, the Russian parliament passed a law forbidding all foreign groups from doing any evangelistic work in Russia. The law made it to President Yeltsin's desk. It was a tense moment for many Christian groups that had already launched tremendous outreach efforts. But through God's grace, President Yeltsin sent back the law.

Spending those days with Billy Graham as he ministered to thousands of people in Russia was a nurturing experience for me. Graham is a gallant, spiritual warrior who has battled sin on many continents. Now he is fighting a personal battle with Parkinson's disease. But no matter how he feels physically, when he stands in front of an audience or a television camera, he seems to come alive and deliver his God-given message with force and zeal. It has been my privilege to have a small part in Billy Graham's dream to reach the world for Christ, sharing with them the message of eternal life.

Day in and day out, working hard
And learning to play the ruthless game,
All the while your heart becomes so cold.
You're selling out your soul,
Reaching for a temporary goal.
But when you reach that final sunset,
And you look into His eyes,

Will the feeling in your heart be joy
Or will it be your last good-bye?
It would be the greatest tragedy
If you never realize that all you own
Cannot compare to eternal life.

You've finally arrived, making lots of money.
But there's emptiness inside,
Spending all your time trying to own the very best
As if somehow the rest will fall in place.

But when you reach that final sunset,
And you look into His eyes
Will the feeling in your heart be joy
Or will it be your last good-bye?
It would be the greatest tragedy
If you never realize that all you own
Cannot compare to eternal life.
And when you reach that final sunset
And the tears well in your eyes,
Will the feeling in your heart be joy

Or will it be your last good-bye?
It would be the greatest tragedy
If you never realize that all you own
Cannot compare to eternal life.

John Stoddard and Wintley Phipps
"Eternal Life"

♪

Chapter 17

Sharing Jesse Jackson's Dreams in Africa

Another dreamer whom God placed in my life is Jesse Jackson. I first heard Jesse Jackson speak when I was a student at Oakwood College. He had been invited to address the students, and even back then in 1973, I was conscious of his exceptional gifts. He was a most dynamic public speaker, and even though two decades have passed since then, I remember the content of his speech and the hope and inspiration it fired within us.

The next time I met Jesse Jackson was when Dr. Frank Hale, the former vice-provost for Ohio State University asked me to sing at a PUSH (People United to Serve Humanity) expo meeting. As I began to sing, Dr. Hale and Jesse Jackson appeared in the doorway of that crowded conference room. I couldn't hear what they were saying, but it appeared that Dr. Hale said, "Jesse, I've got something that I want you to hear."

Then, while I worked on my M.Div. at Andrews University, I visited Jesse Jackson's church and often went to hear him speak. Whenever he saw me there, he invited me to sing.

I was happy to sing for him, but I sensed that my style of singing was not what the PUSH audience was accustomed to.

Jackson was aware of that too, and one day he explained to the audience that for some people music is an expression of soul. For others it is an expression of science. Then in his own inimitable way he shared that my type of singing was a mixture of soul and science. From that time on, the audience accepted me into the PUSH family.

Periodically Jackson invited me to sing at his rallies. It was during my time spent traveling with him that I absorbed much of his wisdom and common sense. One day I accompanied Jackson to Jefferson City, Missouri, where he was to speak at the state legislature. When we arrived in Jefferson City, a car was waiting to take us to the hotel. We had not traveled far when Jackson leaned across to the driver and asked, "Brother, where are we going?"

"Uh, we're going by my house," said the driver, "and then we're stopping at my aunt's house on our way to the hotel."

Realizing that this driver wanted to show off his passengers, Jackson said, "We're going straight to the hotel."

The man looked sheepish and then said, "Okay, we'll go straight to the hotel."

As we sped off in the direction of the hotel, Jackson leaned over to me and said, "Never live your life by someone else's agenda." That little piece of wisdom has guided me toward my dreams.

On another occasion, as we were discussing some gospel singers who were going back and forth from gospel music to secular music, Jackson said to me: "Phipps, you can't ride two horses in the same race." I tucked away that little piece of Jackson wisdom in my mind.

Jackson is always full of surprises. One night as we sat together at a banquet held in Jackson's honor, he suddenly turned to me and asked, "Hey, Phipps, what are you doing next Tuesday?"

"I can't think of anything special I'm doing next Tuesday," I whispered back.

"Well, come to Africa with me," said Jackson.

"Africa!" I exclaimed. "I've never been to Africa."

"Go see Jesse, Jr.," he replied. "He'll give you all the details."

Africa. The word drummed in my brain. Africa. The motherland. I could scarcely wait for the speech to end so that I could slip off the platform and go look for Jesse Jackson, Jr.

"Hey, Jesse, your dad says that I'm going to Africa with you."

"Great," he replied nonchalantly. "Get your passport to me as soon as you can, be sure to have your shots, and start right away on malaria pills."

As soon as I could get to a telephone I called Linda. "Honey. Guess what? I'm going to Africa with Jesse Jackson."

"When?"

"On Tuesday."

"Wow, that's really soon." Linda and I had had many experiences with Jesse Jackson, and we knew that when Jackson has an idea, he moves faster than lightning.

Five days later we flew to London, where we were met and hustled off to a bus bound for Brixton for a meeting with some civic leaders. Driving through the streets of London is always a dream come true for me. From childhood I had cherished picture-book impressions of that historic city of towers and bridges and kings and queens. Through the orderly traffic I glimpsed the red pillar boxes on street corners and tall, old-fashioned street lamps. The London bobbies with their distinctive helmets and batons were something else that I had always longed to see for myself.

As our bus passed Trafalgar Square, someone shouted, "Stop the bus! Stop the bus!" I looked out the window and saw that our bus had stopped directly in front of the South African embassy, where people were holding a protest demonstration. Some were singing, and some were chanting anti-apartheid slogans. In America I had seen similar sights on the newscasts, but this scene was not put on for the television cameras. This protest was for real.

After the Brixton meeting, we flew to Lagos, Nigeria. From there we spent the next three weeks traveling around to view firsthand the effects of apartheid on its neighboring states. Our first stop was at Brazzaville, Congo, and that evening we were the guests of President Negueso at what would be the equivalent of their congress or parliament. After Jackson introduced me, I sang for the gathering. They received me warmly even though I was aware that Seventh-day Adventist churches were having a difficult time in the Congo.

The next day when some of the government officials told me that they enjoyed my singing, I took the opportunity to tell them how sad I was to know that some of my fellow church members were not afforded the same freedom and privileges in their country as I was. I pleaded with the government leaders to do what they could to ease the severe restrictions on my fellow believers in the Congo.

After spending an evening with the U.S. Ambassador to Congo, we flew off to Angola the next morning. I found it disconcerting to step out of the aircraft and find the perimeter of the airport bristling with Soviet aircraft and anti-aircraft guns and behind them a great concentration of military equipment. I had never been so close to anything like it before, and it sent chills up my spine.

"What's going on here?" I asked a baggage inspector.

"It's war, sir," he said. "Angola is at war with South Africa and the CIA-backed guerrillas of Jonas Savembi. All these fortifications are to protect against possible hostilities, sir."

The airport swarmed with soldiers who handled their firearms quite carelessly, pointing them every which way and not making sure the safety catch was on. I felt like saying, "Hey, Brother, take care. Those rifles are lethal weapons."

Instead, I kept as far as possible out of their line of fire, and I breathed a sigh of relief when we got into the vehicles waiting to take the Jackson entourage to our hotel. But I had seen for myself that the Angolans were prepared to fight to the death against forces that they believed threatened their sovereignty.

The next day we attended an ecumenical church service, and at night the Angolan government held a special meeting for the press, in particular the reporters accompanying Jesse Jackson. The Angolan officials displayed one of their South African prisoners of war, an officer named Colonel De Toi. When the press eagerly accepted the opportunity to interview him, Colonel De Toi, a white Afrikaner, spoke courageously. He said that he and his fellow countrymen were willing to fight to the last person to protect what they considered to be their country and the system of apartheid.

It made me feel very sad to hear all these brave men saying that they were ready to die for their different ideologies. What a pity that all peoples of all races cannot live at peace.

On one occasion during the interview, Colonel De Toi made everyone laugh when a reporter asked him whether he had ever heard of Jesse Jackson. "Oh, yes," replied the Colonel. "I have heard of him, and I am glad to see him here. He has had plenty of experience in freeing prisoners of war." The colonel was referring, of course, to Jackson's efforts that had led to the successful release of Lieutenant-Colonel Goodman, the downed American pilot who had been held prisoner by the Syrians.

The next day we flew to Cabinda in North Angola, where we saw Cuban troops protecting Americans who lived and worked on the Chevron Gulf oil fields. Here were Cuban mercenaries protecting Americans from CIA-backed guerrillas who were trying to blow up the oil fields where Americans were working and living. When I tried to understand that complex situation, I was grateful not to be a politician.

From the oil fields we flew back to Luanda, Angola, for a meeting with President Dos Santos and then off to Botswana and after that Mozambique, where we met with the president, General Samora Machel. I was intrigued by this astute man. At one point in the meeting, he fixed his eyes on Jesse Jackson and said, "When you get back to America, remind the American people that they too were once under colonial domination just as we were under Portuguese domination. Remind them that they too had a violent revolution to throw off the colonial yoke. Remind them that they too had a civil war in which brother fought against brother. Also remind them that their first president was a general."

Our next destination was Lusaka in Zambia, where we met President Kenneth Kaunda, an eloquent and emotional orator. The gist of his speech was a warning that because of South Africa's nuclear capability, a sword of destruction hung over the front-line states of southern Africa.

At every stop I was impressed by these amalgamated views of Africa. On television in the United States I had watched huge crowds of men and women in tribal dress, shouting and singing and stamping their feet to express their solidarity; but to see and hear them in real life was something different altogether.

For most of our journey we visited cities that boasted shops, office buildings, schools, and motor vehicles. We met with educated government and professional people with their largely westernized lifestyle. We caught only brief glimpses of the great raw heart of Africa, the simple tribal people living in thatched-hut villages with their dogs and cows and chickens straying all around them. We saw women in bright clothing, hoeing and tending their gardens. Doe-eyed babies bobbed on the backs of others who swung along the dusty roads carrying great baskets of produce on their heads. Barefooted children sang as they guarded grazing cattle, and shawled men gossiped in groups beside narrow trails. Like a continuously running film, sights and sounds and smells assailed our senses in an endless series of vivid scenes.

What a trip it had been. What new vistas it opened up to me. I will always be grateful to Jesse Jackson for allowing me to share his dreams, for introducing me to Africa, and for affording me a perspective on Africa's many problems.

Love is the most durable power in the world. . . .
Love is the only force capable of
transforming an enemy into a friend.

Martin Luther King, Jr.

Chapter 18

Sharing Jesse Jackson's Political Dreams

Jesse Jackson allowed me to share several more of his significant dreams. It seemed to me that when Jackson suspected that something notable was about to happen, he wanted me to be there.

One day in 1984, Jackson called me to say that he wanted me to be at the Democratic National Convention, where he would be nominated as a presidential candidate.

I had a particularly hectic schedule at the time, so I said to him, "If you have something in mind for me to do, let me know. If not, I think I would rather stay home and watch you on television."

Jackson replied, "No, I don't have anything right now, but I'm working on something."

Jesse Jackson has a way of "working" on things. Several weeks later I found myself at the Democratic National Convention in San Francisco. Jackson had arranged for me to sing just before he gave his speech accepting the nomination as a presidential candidate.

The great night came, and we were all rather keyed up and excited. As the evening progressed, it became clear that time was going to be a problem. The people who were introducing Jackson spoke so long that the convention organizers were tense. They eventually rushed into the room where we were all waiting and said, "We must get Jesse on now. It's getting too late at night. We're losing prime time, and people will go to sleep. Quickly, put him up right away."

"What about the song?"

"Scrub the song. Put Jesse up right now." So that was that. I knew that my song was canceled. I wasn't greatly disappointed. I had long ago learned to trust that God was in control. I sat back and relaxed as I listened to Jackson.

Jackson gave a great speech, and when he had finished, the audience went wild. They clapped and waved and whistled, rejoicing because this was the first time in history that a black man had received the honor of being a major candidate for the American presidency.

While the clapping was still going on, Jackson walked over to where I sat on the platform and said, "Hey, what about your song?"

"It was canceled," I said. "They ran out of time."

Jackson shook his head. "Have you got the music?"

"I don't," I replied, somewhat shaken.

"Well, go on anyway. Just hit it. Go on up."

I didn't know what to do. My tape of background music had been sent up to the recording room before the function began, but I didn't know what might have happened to it by now. In the few seconds it took to walk toward the microphone, I debated whether I should wait for music that might not come on, or whether I should sing a cappella. For a brief, nerve-wracking moment I stood at the mike. Then the background music boomed through the audio system. Relief swept over me as I began to sing "God Uses Ordinary People."

In sharing his dream with me, Jesse Jackson also nurtured my dream by giving me an introduction to the national scene.

I received much publicity from singing at Jesse Jackson's nomination. My picture appeared in the Washington Post and other newspapers. My name was mentioned on radio and television. As a direct result, I have made many television appearances and received numerous other invitations to sing.

Anybody can tell you what a world this would be
If we learned to love each other.
I know we would see it, sharing what's in our hearts.
We learn to live together through the stormy weather.
No matter how hard we try,
We've got to keep believing we can make a better world.

Fill the world with love.
Fill the world with joy.
Give what's in your heart.
Fill the world with love.

Shine a light in someone's life; try to make a difference.
Reach down inside your heart, show you really care
Someone may find in you hope for their tomorrow,
And all you did was smile.
It will make you feel God put you there.
You'll believe that you can really.

Fill the world with love.
Fill the world with joy.
Give what's in your heart.
Fill the world with love.

We may not change the world,
But we can give it a fighting chance.
Don't know what tomorrow brings,
But we can make a go of it.
I believe that we can really.

Fill the world with love.
Fill the world with joy.
Give what's in your heart.
Fill the world with love.

♪

Part IV

Dreams Come True

Chapter 19

Making More Albums

My first album, *I Give You My Life*, made in 1978, was a great learning experience. Not only did it cost $20,000, twice as much as I expected, but it was on that album that I figuratively cut my musical teeth.

When I made that first album, I dreamed that God would use it, but I could never have dreamed of the lavish ways he has used it. God's dreams were larger than mine. He has surprised me many times

One night I sang the theme song, "I Give You My Life," in a meeting in Chicago. After the meeting Phil Donahue, the television talk-show host, came up to me and said, simply, "Thank you. I really needed that."

> *Lord, You've given me*
> *More than I could think of,*
> *Lord, You've given me*
> *More than I could dream of,*
> *Lord, You've given me more than my full share.*

> *Lord, You've given me Your all*
> *I give you my life,*
> *Please hear me pray, dear Lord,*
> *I give You my life,*
> *Don't let me stray, dear Lord,*
> *I give You my life,*
> *Please take it and use it Lord, to Your will.*

Never did I dream that the life and music I gave to the Lord in that album would be used to touch thousands of people through the years.

Not everything went smoothly in those early days. In my inexperience, sometimes I did not have legal counsel when I signed contracts. At one point I signed an agreement with a recording company before I really understood what it was all about. Too late I found out that by signing that document, I had lost all rights to my first two albums, *I Give You My Life* and *Lord, You Are My Music.*

From then on I could not record any of the songs on these albums without asking someone else's permission. Even though I had composed these songs myself, songs like "My Child" and "Remember Me," they were no longer mine. I almost wept. I was surely learning some hard lessons about life in the music business.

The passage of time did little to heal my hurt. I think I felt it all the more deeply because it was my fault. It is always comforting to be able to blame someone else when things go wrong. But this was entirely my fault. I should have been wise enough to read the fine print and if I didn't understand some of it, to ask for an explanation.

I guess the wound was still smarting when I told Mr. George Johnson of Johnson Products in Chicago about the whole sad story. One day he telephoned me. "Wintley, the Lord has told me that you should write to those people and ask them to give you back your music."

I gasped. This was an unheard of thing to do. Once a copyright is sold, it is sold. Stories abound of penniless poets and writers who sold their work for a pittance only to learn that the buyer made a fortune from it. These thoughts flashed through my mind faster than it takes to tell them, and I was about to protest, when another thought struck me. If God had spoken to Mr. Johnson, I should do as he said.

"All right, Mr. Johnson," I said. "If the Lord has given you this message for me, I'll do it." As I hung up the phone, my thoughts were in turmoil. What would I say? A contract is a contract. But if it was God's idea, then I should do it.

I prayed about it, and that night I sat down and composed one of the most difficult letters I've ever written. I made no demands and no pleas. Instead, I explained that I had not been fully aware of the implications that signing the document entailed. I explained how much these songs meant to me and how I wanted to use them in my ministry.

The prompt reply that I received was what my weak faith had fully expected. In essence it said, You must be crazy. We don't give back music that we have paid for.

Anger welled up inside me. I felt my blood pressure rise as indignation fought disappointment. How dare they?

Linda took the letter from my clenched fist and read it. "It's their right to do that, Wintley," she said. Her soft voice melted my anger.

I turned toward the telephone, ready to call Mr. Johnson and read him the letter, but something seemed to stop me. I got a distinct impression that everything wasn't over yet.

Three weeks later I received another letter from the record company. Apparently the person who wrote the first letter had given a copy of it to his superior. The superior wrote:

Mr. Phipps, we don't often do this, but in your case we are willing to sell back to you all rights and ownership of your first album for $5,000. For a further $5,000 we will also return all rights and ownership of your second album.

All I could say as I read the letter was, "Praise God."

With Mr. Johnson's help, I bought back all the rights of my first two albums and learned a priceless lesson in the process. To me this experience exemplified the process of redemption. I composed those songs. I sang them. Then I foolishly unwittingly sold them. By a miracle of God, I was able to buy them back again.

Isn't that what Jesus has done for us? He made us. We belong to him. Then we foolishly sold out to sin and Satan. But Jesus paid with his own shed blood to buy us back again. We are redeemed.

Not everyone understood my dream either. Some record companies that I thought were interested in my music wanted me to compromise my message before they would consider a contract. I had decided in the beginning that I would not compromise, even if that meant that no one would record my albums.

While I became discouraged when that happened, God gave me direction. Once while flying back from Los Angeles, after pursuing a false lead on a record contract, God spoke to me: "You are my child. And my children should never have to stand before the Devil's kingdom and petition the Devil to get my message out or help make their dreams come true. That's like going to Herod and asking him to help you find the baby Jesus. Herod didn't want to find Jesus; he wanted to kill him."

So many of the people to whom we go to help make our dreams come true are not in the business of discovering or sharing the majesty of Jesus. Their agenda is altogether different.

God said, "I'm speaking to you just as I spoke to those three wise men. I'm telling you to go home another way. Find your dream only in me."

God's counsel to me meant that even if the only albums I would make would be made in my living room, with my son holding the microphone and my wife strumming a guitar, then we would make music. By the grace of God I had to be willing to make my own music and go it alone.

My third album, *I Choose You Again*, came out of that determination to go ahead and make music without the aid of a record company. I used the emerging technology of computer sampling to provide all the orchestral sounds I could not afford. As soon as I heard about this innovation and saw it demonstrated, I realized the possibilities. With Mr. George Johnson's help I bought my first computer sampler. The quality of the background music was convincing. Many people thought that all of my songs were accompanied by a full complement of live musicians, but they were not. I had the invaluable help of Jerry Bowles, an extremely talented young man, who produced and orchestrated each song.

I also did my fourth album, *We Are One*, by myself. I paid all the expenses, even hiring a full orchestra this time to accompany the songs. On this album I recorded a song called "Thank You, America," which was used for the celebrations of the reopening of the Statue of Liberty. It was recorded on the Statue of Liberty album, along with music done by John Williams, Sandi Patti, Glen Campbell, and others. I was the only non-American to sing on this album. It was my way of saying thank you to my adoptive country.

Thank you, America, for all that freedom means to me;
Thank you, America, for freedom of faith and liberty.

The fifth album, *Wintley Phipps*, came about when Dan Johnson, one of the vice-presidents at Word Records, a Christian recording company based in Dallas, Texas, became interested in my music. Johnson believed in what God had been doing in my music ministry. He almost single-handedly made this album happen. My first Grammy nomination came from this album.

On the sixth album, *A Love Like This*, I recorded a song called "The Potter," which, of all the songs I have written, was the one my mother liked best. It ministered to her as she lay dying of cancer. It spoke to her of the hope that one day God the Potter would make over her ailing body.

I recorded a Christmas album, *It's Christmas Time*, because my wife, Linda, felt strongly that I should do it. I made the album, not knowing who would be touched by it. As always, God's plans are not our own. I was told that Diana Ross wants to record the title song, which I wrote, on her new Christmas album.

The Great Controversy, the eighth album, is a musical about the story of redemption, from the interaction between Adam and Eve in the Garden, to the Crucifixion, to Christ's coming again. One song I particularly enjoy on that album, "Keep on Climbing," expresses my deeply felt sentiments about how God moves mountains to make our dreams come true.

My experience with my ninth album, *The Sun Will Shine Again*, proved to me again that God honors our dreams when we refuse to compromise his will for us. One of the songs on this album is a duet. When we were preparing the album, Linda and I considered who would be good for that duet. Linda had a wonderful idea. "Wintley, I think Patti Labelle would be perfect for the duet. What do you think?"

"I agree she would be a great choice. She has an incredible gift. But she probably wouldn't be interested in singing on a gospel album," I responded.

Never one to give up, Linda encouraged me, "Well, why don't you call and find out?"

When I called Patti Labelle's husband, who is her manager, he said, "She's not doing any duets right now, but something tells me that she's really going to like this song." He called back a few weeks later and said, "Patti really wants to do this."

"You're kidding!" I said.

"No, I don't kid about these things," he assured me.

When I talked with Patti Labelle, I told her how grateful I was that she would do the duet with me. She responded, "I'm honored to do this."

"No," I countered, "I'm the one who's honored."

My interactions with Patti Labelle and her husband taught me an important lesson. They treated me in ways that allowed me to see Christ. Their respect, grace, kindness, and love blessed me immensely. I realized that their actions outshined the treatment many Christians give each other.

The tenth album, *The Power of a Dream*, will be released before the end of 1994, a musical companion story to this book.

In all of these albums, I have written and sung to the glory of God, praying that he will use the words and music to touch the hearts of people and turn them to him. Two of these albums, *A Love like This* and *Wintley Phipps*, were nominated to receive the Grammy award. Although I did not win a Grammy in either case, I was honored to be considered along with the other singers and musicians. But even that honor I keep in proper perspective. Long ago God showed me that he measures success not by billboard charts, units sold, gate takings, or applause meters; God judges the heart, our inner motives and thoughts, our passion for his will and his work.

Dream and deed are not as differed as many think.
All the deeds of men are dreams at first,
and become deeds in the end.

Theodore Herzl
Postscripts

♪

Chapter 20

Opportunities in Television

Through the years God has given me many wonderful opportunities to witness for him through the medium of television—from appearing on *Saturday Night Live* to singing in Christmas specials to hosting talk shows.

My first experience with hosting television programs began in Baltimore, Maryland. For two years I co-hosted a one-hour, community-based talk show known as *Sunday Live*. From that shaky beginning I progressed to other shows, and slowly I began to feel more comfortable with television. I later hosted a weekly talk show, *New Horizons*, on the Black Entertainment Television network, and a weekly half-hour program called *Stellar Showcase*.

As I accepted invitations to appear on television, I worried a lot about whether I could sing my type of music. But even when appearing on *Saturday Night Live*, one of television's most popular comedy shows, it presented no problem. Again God showed me that I did not have to compromise the message in my songs to be recognized.

After singing at a service one Saturday morning, I walked into Jesse Jackson's PUSH operation's office and saw a man sitting alone. He was neatly but plainly dressed in slacks and sweater. He certainly gave no evidence of either wealth or importance. After we exchanged greetings, he began questioning me, probing more deeply than the usual superficial inquiries one makes when trying to become acquainted with someone. I wondered why he was so curious about me. I told him who I was and why I was at Jesse's office. When some of Jesse's supporters came into the room, our conversation ended. That was the end of the incident as far as I was concerned.

A few weeks later I received a phone call. "Good morning, Wintley. This is George Johnson. I met you at Jesse Jackson's office, remember? My brother has passed away, and I would like you to come and sing at his funeral." I obliged and again I thought that was the end of the matter.

I didn't know at that time that George Johnson was the creative man who, with only a few hundred dollars capital, founded the Johnson Products Company, which brought to black Americans such products as Ultra Sheen, Afro Sheen, and a host of innovative and successful hair-care products. I also didn't know at the time how much this man would come to mean to me and how much he would contribute to the dreams God had planned for me.

Several months later George Johnson called again. "Wintley, I've been thinking. You know that song of yours 'I Give You My Life'? I'd like to hear you sing that on *Soul Train*. Would you do it?"

"I'd be happy to sing it on *Soul Train*," I said, but I thought to myself, *How on earth does he think he would get me, a gospel singer, onto* Soul Train? *Their music is anything but religious. They are interested more in the rock artists and soul groups than in a preacher who sings.*

"I'll ask Don Cornelius to put you on," he said and hung up. Needless to say, Don Cornelius, the host of *Soul Train* was anything but enthusiastic about having a gospel singer appear on his show. But Johnson was persuasive. "Now listen, Don. You have so many young people on your show, all dressed up funny and dancing around. What this young man is trying to say in his music is important. Those are the very young people who ought to hear his message." Cornelius was not convinced. He did not want anything religious on his show.

Again Johnson argued passionately that I should appear on *Soul Train*. Again Don Cornelius refused. "That's not my type of show," he said obstinately.

Apparently God as well as Mr. Johnson wanted me to appear on *Soul Train*, because while this dialogue was going on, the news broke that the ailing singer Minnie Ripperton had just died of cancer.

A day or two later I received a phone call. "Don Cornelius here," a voice said. "We would like to have you appear on *Soul Train*."

"That will be all right," I said, "as long as you are willing to let me sing my kind of music."

Cornelius replied, "I know that. Give me time to think. We're going to have to make a special show, something unique that will fit in with your type of music."

Within hours Don Cornelius was back to me. "I've got it," he said. "I guess you've heard about Minnie Ripperton? We'll put on a special show as a tribute to Minnie. That way we can do something serious without losing our audience. You and Stevie Wonder will be the musical guests."

During the remainder of that call and several more that followed, we resolved the details of my part in the program. Contrary to Don Cornelius' expectations, the gospel music and the serious program put on in memory of Minnie Ripperton were well received.

Mr. Johnson's influence did not end with getting me on *Soul Train*. He involved me in a gospel-music variety show called "Stellar Showcase," which was sponsored by the Johnson Products Company. George Johnson also happened to be a member of Robert Schuller's board of directors. He talked to Schuller and suggested that he have me sing on his television program.

Through George Johnson's kindness and consistent mentoring, I had many opportunities to sing on television. I have never taken those opportunities lightly. I have always felt under obligation to share my ministry and to do my best. Perhaps this stems from my deep conviction that television is the most powerful socializing influence of our day. Television has become the primary communication vehicle of our time. To fail to use it often and well is to lose precious opportunities to make a positive difference in our world.

Vision is the art of seeing things invisible.

Jonathan Swift
Thoughts on Various Subjects

♪

Chapter 21

Singing in Rome

When the Lord fulfilled my dreams to be a singer, he also fulfilled many other dreams. He allowed me to travel widely and represent both him and the American Christian community as an ambassador of music.

I was in Rome to sing with a delegation of American musical goodwill ambassadors who were performing gospel music in several of Rome's holy shrines and basilicas. The event was a first in the great city of the Caesars, at least in recent history, and our group bubbled with excitement. We were all thrilled to be a part of this great ecumenical adventure.

We arrived in Rome on a glorious spring day: Linda, Wintley II, and I; the Hawkins family from Oakland, California; Danibelle Hall; and several Catholic and Protestant groups from the Baltimore area. Our first rehearsal went well. Then we all piled into a huge coach, and a guide took us to see some of the famous sights of the eternal city. As we went from one place to another, we saw placards and advertising banners announcing the arrival of the gospel singers from America.

Our hosts graciously drove us around the impressive Capitoline Hill and across many of the bridges that span the famous Tiber River. We saw the Colosseum, where many Christian martyrs gave their lives for their faith; the Pantheon; the Fontana di Trevi, perhaps best known of all Rome's beautiful fountains; and countless massive churches and public buildings.

The next morning the coach took all of us to the presidential palace to meet various officials. We waited in the huge reception hall with its carpeting worth a king's ransom and its breathtaking treasures of art and sculpture. We scarcely dared to speak above a whisper in the presence of such magnificence.

Once again little Wintley's smile proved to open doors. As I remember, he was the only child in the group, and he soon attracted the attention of the president's wife. Mrs. Fanfani snatched him up and fussed over him. Our little family quickly became the center of her attention, rather to the dismay of others in the group, who were far more worthy.

At lunch time, when our whole group was whisked off to eat at an outdoor restaurant, Mrs. Fanfani insisted that Linda, Wintley II, and I sit at her table as her special guests. After lunch we were driven back to the presidential palace for a formal audience with President Fanfani. Again we waited in the magnificent reception hall until the doors swung open and the president himself strode in to meet our group.

President Fanfani was a short, distinguished-looking man with an engaging smile. At the end of all the usual introductions and exchange of pleasantries, he asked us to give him a preview of the program that we had prepared for the people of Rome. The president appeared pleased with what he heard.

As we left the palace and headed back for afternoon rehearsals, our guide informed us that arrangements had already been made for the next day's program. We were to sing during the early morning religious ceremony in St. Peter's

Square, and we were to have an audience with the pope. That really sent a ripple of excitement through our group, some of whom were Roman Catholics.

The next morning the gospel singers lined up close to where Pope John Paul II would appear. Because we stood on an elevated platform, we could look across the great sea of humanity that had gathered there. Never have I seen such a congregation. Never will I forget the kaleidoscope of color as those thousands on thousands of tourists and worshipers pressed tightly into St. Peter's Square, waiting for what I guess most of them judged to be the greatest event of their lives.

Presently a swelling murmur of voices and the sound of applause swept through the crowd as the papal entourage appeared. A moment earlier people had been pushing and jostling to gain a better view, but when Pope John Paul II halted and raised his hand in blessing, a hushed stillness settled over the vast throng. I was amazed to see so much adoration and adulation centered on one human being.

The pope recited the mass in a firm voice, and the crowd responded reverently at the appropriate pauses. Afterward the pope greeted the people in a number of different languages. It was easy to see that this gesture made him even more popular.

At various stages of the proceedings, the gospel singers sang the songs we had prepared. By the time the ceremonies ended, the sun was high overhead, its beams glinting off the gold and jewelry worn by pope and prelates. Medieval Swiss guards in their black hats and red-and-yellow-striped doublets stood rigidly at attention while camera-toting tourists flocked to take pictures of them. Small Italian boys darted in and out among the crowd, selling souvenirs and postcards.

Eventually the pope stepped down to walk among the people. At that time security was much more relaxed than it has been since the attempt was made on his life. As he mingled with the worshipers, I noticed one of the aides whisper in the pope's ear and point in our direction. Immediately the pope turned in our direction. "He's coming over to us," the woman standing next to me in the crowd whispered excitedly. Because of the dense throng the pope's progress was slow, and I didn't think he would do more than greet us as a group.

But to my surprise, after being introduced to our leader, he systematically greeted each person. When it came my turn, I extended my hand. He shook it, and I felt the warm softness of his fingers and the cold metal of his special ring. He paused momentarily, and as I looked directly into his eyes, I got the impression that despite the warmth and friendliness of his smile, he was a man with an iron will.

> *Delight yourself in the Lord*
> *and he will give you*
> *the desires of your heart.*
>
> *Psalm 37:4*

♪

Chapter 22

Traveling Behind
The Iron Curtain

When I turned my life over to the Lord and gave him my dreams, one of my dearest wishes was to travel. I wasn't sure whether that would fit in with his plans for my life, so I put that dream on the altar with the others. God's provision is so abundant, that when I look back on my life, I am overwhelmed. The Lord's dream for me took the little boy who wrote imaginary destinations on red-and-white luggage tags from the Montreal airport to places he never dreamed he would travel: Bombay, Beijing, Belfast, Brisbane.

In 1974, not long before Linda and I became engaged, I was invited to go to Vienna and be the gospel soloist in a crusade with J. Malcolm Phipps, a U.S.-born evangelist. Not only do we share the same last name but his grandfather, Fred C. Phipps, was a charter member of the very first Adventist Church in Trinindad.

After our series of evangelistic meetings ended, I stayed on a little longer. I wanted to see something of Europe, and above all I wanted to go behind the Iron Curtain. World War II history and memorabilia fascinate me. I can sit for hours and read about the battles fought during that terrible conflict and listen to the speeches of Sir Winston Churchill. I can watch old World War II movies one after another and not become bored with them. It simply astounds me how one man driven by madness and evil could turn the entire world upside down. So with that interest driving me, I wanted to use the opportunity to visit some of the countries that were engulfed in that war in the 1940s.

I stood in line for hours to obtain a visa to Czechoslovakia. I have never known a line to move as slowly as that one did. I couldn't see any red tape, but I'm sure that every clerk in that office was bound hand and foot in miles of it. When finally I got the visa and changed some money to pay for an entrance permit, I joined another line waiting to cross the border from the West to the East.

Literally trembling with nervousness, I watched those in front of me submit to having their luggage and their clothing searched. I was so nervous that I had to take tight hold of myself. I didn't want any of those cold-eyed guards seeing me wipe my sweaty palms.

My main concern was that I might be searched. I had in my pocket a small Bible that I didn't want the guards to find. I knew that Bibles were not allowed in communist countries, but I never travel anywhere without a copy of the Scriptures. To my relief, apart from a perfunctory patting of pockets, I was not searched at the crossing point. But they went over my papers so thoroughly that I began to wonder whether I had been given forged permits. My fears almost changed to anger by the time I had waited for half an hour while they read every word of small print and minutely studied every entry in my passport.

Eventually I left the last border guard behind and reached the city of Bratislava in the former Czechoslovakia. For hours I roamed the empty streets and looked at monuments and intricately carved, unused churches. The streets were deserted except for an occasional subdued-looking bird hopping across the cobblestones.

There were so few people in the streets that Bratislava seemed like a city spent and exhausted by the struggle to survive. The occasional person I met ignored my presence. If I saw someone approaching, I watched expectantly, ready to give a greeting or at least a smile. But as we passed each other, the person kept his or her eyes averted. Everyone mistrusted everyone else, and I was so obviously a foreigner that they doubly distrusted me.

Once or twice I passed shops: a bakery displaying a few loaves of white bread and a grocery store with shelves almost bare of commodities. Inside the shops stood the lines of silent, shawled, expressionless women waiting patiently to buy a few necessities.

I found it chilling, both emotionally and physically, to be behind the Iron Curtain. Every aspect was cold and gray and depressing. I felt an atmosphere of hopelessness so tangible that it settled on my shoulders and pressed down on my spirit. I wandered around the streets until my time was up, and I admit to breathing a sigh of relief when I recrossed the border into Austria.

The atmosphere in Austria was refreshingly different, like a cold shower after a rugged football game. I loved the stately buildings and the Old World air that pervaded the cities on the outside. Inside, everything was as modern as American shops and offices. The clock and watch shops particularly fascinated me. Never in my life had I seen such a variety of timepieces ticking and tocking, dinging and donging, striking and chiming. It was in Austria that I bought the engagement watch for Linda.

Since those first exciting trips abroad, I have traveled extensively in Africa with Jesse Jackson. I have conducted several singing evangelism campaigns in the United Kingdom and in the great southland, Australia. I have been to Russia with Billy Graham, and I have been to islands in the South Seas. The Lord delights in giving us the desires of our hearts.

> *Where there is no vision, the people perish.*
> *Proverbs 29:18 (KJV)*

♪

Chapter 23

Dreams Touch Others

Many times God uses our dreams to touch others. I remember one trip, when Linda, Wintley II, and I were standing at the airlines counter in Los Angeles, waiting for seat assignments. The clerk was doing a great deal of click-clacking on her computer and looking more anxious by the minute. Finally she looked up at me and said, "I'm sorry, sir, but there are no non-smoking seats left in coach."

"I'm sorry too," I replied, "but we *must* travel in a non-smoking area. I am a singer on my way to a concert, and I can't risk having my throat irritated by tobacco smoke."

"I understand." The clerk smiled briefly and turned back to her computer. She did a little more key clicking and then wrote out seat numbers for us. As she handed them to me, she said, "You'll have to sit in first class. There are no other non-smoking seats available on this flight."

I thanked her, and we made our way on to the plane. For the first hour or so little Wintley sat quietly enough, overawed by the new surroundings and the novelty of the airplane. Then he became restless. He clambered all over Linda and me, accidentally kicking the back of the seats in front of us and bothering the people there who were trying to doze. We tried every way to amuse him and keep him sitting still, but five hours can be a long, long time to a small boy.

"Take him for a walk," Linda whispered to me. "He needs to stretch his legs."

I took his hand and walked with him up and down the aisles in the first-class cabin. Wintley was about three years old at the time and had a friendly disposition. He smiled at all the people we passed, and they smiled back, spoke to him, patted his head. His lack of guile completely won their hearts.

One woman in particular attracted his attention. Wintley halted right in front of her and smiled. She smiled back and began to play a little game of peek-a-boo with him. I stood back and watched, wondering where I had seen this woman before. Her face looked familiar, yet I didn't think she was anyone I knew personally. Presently she looked around at me and smiled and then I recognized her. She was Natalie Wood.

When I took Wintley back to Linda, I reached into my bag for a copy of my first album, *I Give You My Life*. Then I walked back along the aisle and knelt down beside Natalie Wood's seat. "I feel impressed to give you this," I said. "The kind of music I sing is gospel music, and I would like you to listen to the whole album. If you don't have time for that, I particularly want you to hear the title song 'I Give You My Life.' It's a song of commitment and consecration to God."

"Thank you." She flashed me a smile. "I always carry a cassette recorder when I travel. I will listen to your album as we fly."

When we landed at Atlanta, Natalie Wood was one of the first passengers off the plane, and I thought that was the end of the episode. By the time we had gathered up our hand baggage and our small son, we were among the last to disembark. Imagine my surprise to see Natalie Wood waiting for us at the jetway. She shook my hand and looked up at me with shining eyes, "Thank you so much." She squeezed my hand in goodbye. "God bless you."

I never saw her again. Days later the newspapers screamed the headlines: *Natalie Wood drowned.*

I firmly believe that God allowed our paths to cross and gave me the opportunity to witness to this beautiful woman at a very crucial moment in her life.

Only he who can see the invisible can do the impossible.

Frank Gaines
Forbes

♪

Chapter 24

Singing for Diana Ross

I first came to know Diana Ross as the result of a television program on which I sang. I sang "Tell Me Again," a song that I had written when needing God's assurance that he still loved me. When she heard the song, she was so moved that she wept. Immediately after the show ended, she called her secretary and said, "Find that guy."

I knew nothing about any of this until one morning I answered my telephone and heard a crisp voice say, "I'm calling for Diana Ross. She would like you to sing at her wedding in Geneva, Switzerland."

I was shocked dumb. Diana Ross! After a few seconds of hard swallowing, I managed to croak, "When?" After the secretary told me the date and time and after I checked my schedule, I replied, "Yes, I think I can make it."

She replied, "Okay, then. I'll book your flight and make your hotel reservations right away. Your tickets will be waiting for you at the airport."

I put the telephone down and sat staring at it. Was this really true, or was someone playing a joke on me? I had no way of knowing. Every few days I called the airlines to check whether my ticket was really prepaid. Or I would call to order a vegetarian meal for my flight. Or I would call to check departure time or arrival time, anything to try to convince myself that this was not one of my childhood dreams. It wasn't. This was a dream about to come true.

The wedding took place in a small town outside Geneva. Obviously money was of no consequence to the husband-to-be, Arne Naess, a Norwegian shipping magnate. He arranged for a boys' choir to fly to Geneva to take part in the ceremony. The guest list included famous people from all over the world, including Gregory Peck and Stevie Wonder. The hotels overflowed with celebrities.

Diana Ross could have had any of the great names perform at her wedding, but she chose me, someone she had never met. It was almost unbelievable.

Graham Ferguson Lacy, the minister who conducted the ceremony was a friend of Arne's. Lacy and I stayed at the same hotel and attended the rehearsal together.

The wedding was to be held in a quaint stone church where I could almost see monks from the twelfth century in their rusty habits and smell the incense that they carried. Ross, effervescent and joyfully excited, came up to me at the rehearsal. It was our first meeting. "What do you think you will sing?" she asked. I suggested "The Lord's Prayer" and "The Twenty-Third Psalm," and she agreed. "But I would like one more," she said. I was not sure what else to suggest, so I told her about "Love Divine," a song I had written and sung for Linda at our wedding. "Please sing it for me."

Right there in that old church in Switzerland, I sang for Diana Ross. When I finished, her eyes were filled with tears. "That's just the song," she said.

After Ross went off to attend to other plans, Graham Lacy walked up to me and said, "Brother, I can see that you are a Christian."

"A striving Christian," I said, and we smiled and embraced each other.

Lacy told me that when he was invited to perform the ceremony, he had felt he would be in an alien environment among all these celebrities. "I knew I would be like a fish out of water, so I prayed that the Lord would send someone to whom I could relate, and he has. I'm so glad you are here, Wintley."

Graham then told me of his background. He and Arne had been friends in the business world until Graham was converted and decided to become a Christian minister. "When I was invited to come here and perform the wedding ceremony, I hoped that I would meet a brother with whom I could share my love for God."

Perhaps drawn by our mutual love for the Lord, Graham and I became good friends. Many months later, when he was married at the Anglican church at Oxford in England, he paid my fare to go over and sing at his wedding.

Lacy's wedding was also a grand affair. The reception was held in Blenheim Palace, ancestral home of the Duke of Marl-borough. I particularly remember the dozens of Grenadier guards that entertained the guests with formation marching to stirring band music. They looked wonderful with a spotlight shining down on their scarlet coats and bearskin headdresses.

Millionaires and billionaires from all over the world were at that wedding. During the post-reception chatter one of them strolled up to Graham and said, "I wonder whether Wintley would be interested in coming to Australia and singing in some television commercials that we are about to make."

As Graham listened to the details of the proposal, he answered for me. "No," he said positively. "I know Wintley well enough to say that his integrity would not allow him to sing for your breweries' commercials."

I have never conceded the integrity of the messages in my songs, but I have sung them in places where many long for the privilege and opportunity of doing so. I have sung in the strangest places, sometimes to millions of people, sometimes to just a handful. God has fulfilled my dreams beyond my wildest imaginings.

> *To accomplish great things,*
> *we must not only act but also dream,*
> *not only plan but also believe.*
>
> Anatole France

♪

Chapter 25

The Heartbreak of South Africa

It all began with a phone call from one of Jesse Jackson's staff members. "Jesse wants you to accompany him to South Africa," she said. "Can you leave next week?"

Of course I said yes. Jesse Jackson has a keen instinct for the historic. He seems to have some inner sense of timing that warns him when something special is about to happen.

No one knew exactly when Nelson Mandela was to be released from prison. The day and hour were a closely guarded state secret. But Jesse Jackson had a hunch that it would be soon, very soon, and he wanted to be there.

Our flight was uneventful, but the moment we alighted from the plane in Johannesburg, South Africa, I felt the excitement. The air seemed to crackle with tension. The officials who met us at Jan Smuts airport said little. They whisked us away to a reception hosted by Dr. Frank Chikane of the South African Council of Churches. The reception was held in the SACC's recently opened headquarters, occupied after their building had been destroyed by a powerful bomb two years earlier.

The speeches were well under way when I noticed a distinguished looking gray-haired man enter the room. "That's Dr. Sisulu," the man on my right whispered. "He spent twenty-five years in prison," he added in a reverent undertone.

"Uh huh." I nodded. I had heard Jesse Jackson speak of Dr. Sisulu, who had spent so much of his life with Nelson Mandela in the infamous Robben Island Prison. For the first fifteen years of their imprisonment they were not allowed to see a newspaper. Two more years passed before either of them was allowed to touch his wife's hand when she visited.

And what was their heinous crime? Simply that they had dared to fight for their dreams of a South Africa where all of God's children, black or white, could live in peace, equality, and freedom.

I watched the respect accorded to Dr. Sisulu. People spoke to or of him in reverential tones. Being an ex-prisoner in South Africa was not something to be ashamed of. Rather the experience was a badge of distinction to be worn with dignity and quiet pride. Imprisonment for this cause made a man a hero.

The next morning we were to meet with many of the prominent clergy of Johannesburg. As our convoy traveled to the meeting place, I noticed that the windows of Jackson's vehicle were unusually thick. When I remarked on it, Jackson chuckled. "That's bullet-proof glass, Wintley. It's an armor-plated car that weighs more than a one-ton truck." That was when I learned that radicals had made threats against Jesse Jackson's life if he came to South Africa. His hosts were taking no chances.

The inspiration of those breakfast speeches and prayers helped to prepare me for our visit to Soweto, a bustling black township not far from Johannesburg. I suppose Soweto could be looked on as a city of refuge. Over four million dispossessed black people live there, many forced out of their former homes by apartheid. Some of them live in shacks made from cardboard and galvanized aluminum, some no wider than six feet.

Many people in Soweto have no running water, no electricity, no plumbing, no garbage collection. One hospital serves the entire community of four million people; little wonder that scores of patients sleep on ward floors and others wait for hours at outpatient departments staffed by harried nurses and overworked doctors.

Despite the squalor of their surroundings, the people expressed a quiet dignity. For the most part they are buoyed up by hope and their determination to be free. This is their country, and they want to possess it.

Our next visit was to Cape Town, one of the most beautiful cities in Africa. After Soweto, Cape Town seemed like heaven. Azure sky reflected in foam-capped sea. Table Mountain was draped in a cloth of snowy cloud. Orderly streets of well-kept homes and colorful gardens gave a pervading sense of peace and prosperity.

Even in Cape Town it was impossible to ignore South Africa's problems. Even though we did not hear many people actively discuss apartheid, we got the impression that intense feelings lay just beneath the surface, like gunpowder waiting for an igniting spark to set it off. Both races had what they thought were reasonable, logical arguments to support their particular point of view. Only in extreme instances could the issue be termed black or white. In most cases, there were so many gray areas of disagreement that the issues seem as if they would never be solved.

Our visit to Soweto had prepared me somewhat for our trip to Crossroads, where sixty thousand people struggle to survive in unlit slums. When our vehicles arrived, the people hurriedly passed word around that the country preacher had come to Crossroads. Within minutes several thousand people gathered. They sang, they chanted, they clapped hands, and stamped feet in a *toi-toi* dance of celebration as Jackson mounted a makeshift pulpit in the open air and began to speak to them.

As Jackson spoke of hope and determination, I watched the faces of the people nearest to me. A spark of interest illumined their sullen faces. When Jackson concluded, they came alive with a vigor they had not shown before. They shouted *"Amandla, Amandla"* and clapped and threw dust in the air. "Tomorrow!" they chanted. "Tomorrow! Mandela will be released. Tomorrow!" The words acted like a stimulant on the crowd. They swayed and sweated, waving arms and shouting, "Tomorrow! It will be tomorrow." The thudding of their stamping feet took on a triumphant rhythm.

I wondered whether they knew something that we didn't know, or was their prediction merely symbolic? If it was true, I marveled anew that Jackson's instinct had brought us to South Africa at such a momentous time.

As our convoy sped away from Crossroads, we somehow lost touch with Jackson's vehicle. We stopped and someone suggested we turn back and look for him. Several vehicles turned back, and as we reached the outskirts of Crossroads, a woman ran toward us, frantically waving and shouting, "The police. The police. They've teargassed the crowd, and now they're shooting."

Shocked into inaction, we saw a group of women appear out of the choking cloud, coughing, sputtering, and staggering under their burden, the blood-stained body of a man.

Before we collected our dazed senses, a long yellow truck pulled up in front of our vehicle and a dozen blue-shirted police piled out. Using their rifle butts as clubs, they cleared the road of people and told us to get going. Our driver needed no second telling, and we sped back the way we had come, horrified by our firsthand encounter with the brutality of apartheid.

Sunday morning, I was with Jesse Jackson's group in Cape Town to witness the release of Nelson Mandela, the Mahatma

Gandhi of South Africa. Words are inadequate to express my feelings as I saw this dignified man, looking remarkably fit for his seventy-two years, address the great crowd of people waiting to hear him speak publicly for the first time in a quarter of a century.

Think of it. Nelson Mandela, a man who has literally suffered himself into power. A man who, without a missile or a standing army, without a title or a political office, has become the most powerful man in South Africa today.

The majority of the people who live in South Africa regard him as their leader. When he speaks, the world listens.

One of the greatest miracles is that Nelson Mandela came out of prison without a trace of bitterness or thirst for revenge. He even refers to his jailer as his friend and says that through the long years he was sustained by faith and prayer. In South Africa one can only marvel at the ability of an oppressed people to absorb suffering without bitterness.

Nelson Mandela's first night of freedom was spent at Bishop Desmond Tutu's home. The next day our party joined them for lunch, and I met Mrs. Winnie Mandela. Later in the day we met with then-President De Klerk and Minister Pik Botha. Reflecting on those days, what joy it was to see Nelson Mandela take the oath and be sworn in as the newly elected President of South Africa. South Africa is one of the most enchanting and beautiful countries in the world. May God bless its land and people with peace.

But the bravest are surely those
who have the clearest vision of what is before them,
glory and danger alike, and notwithstanding
go out and meet it.

Thucydides
Funeral Oration of Pericles

♪

Chapter 26

Surviving a Plane Crash

My unexpected trip to South Africa to witness the release of Nelson Mandela forced me to reschedule some of my appointments back home. One of these was in Spokane, Washington.

After church I dashed to the airport to catch a flight from Baltimore to Seattle, making it with not a minute to spare. Because my schedule was so tight, my host kindly rented a private plane to take me from Seattle to Spokane. I'm not a nervous person, but I don't believe in taking unnecessary risks, particularly not now that I have a wife and sons depending on me. I requested a twin-engine plane, and as we hurried across the tarmac at Seattle, I was relieved to find that the private plane waiting for us was a six-seater twin-engine Cessna, complete with radar and other sophisticated equipment.

My host assured me that the pilot had many hours of flying experience and that the other man with him was a fellow pilot. I nodded, and we hurried to board the Cessna. I did not begin any work because this was going to be only a short flight, time enough for me to have some time for prayer and consecration.

As the little plane rose like a bird into the clear blue sky, it soared over the Cascade Mountains. I looked down, awe-struck by the sight of unending miles of snow-crowned ridges sparkling in the sunlight. My heart throbbed with love for my Creator and Redeemer, and I strongly felt God's presence in the tiny cabin. I began to think of all the wonderful things that God had done for me. *Lord,* I said in my mind, *why are you so good to me? I know I don't deserve it.*

A more than usual sense of peace settled over me. I felt entirely relaxed and in communion with God. As I prayed and reflected on God's leading in my life, his goodness and mercy, and the wonderful way in which he had blessed me with far more than I could have asked or thought, I sensed the Lord was speaking to me. "No matter what happens, Son, I will take care of you."

I wondered why he said that. Then I opened my eyes and immediately became aware that while I had been meditating, basking in the light of God's love and assurances, the sunshine had disappeared. Dark clouds billowed angrily around us, and a drizzling rain spat at the windows.

The plane began to rock and buck. Almost at the same time I saw the lights of Spokane appear below us in the gloom. A moment later they disappeared again.

The pilot spoke to the air-traffic control tower and lined up his approach. We circled and began to descend more smoothly than I expected, considering the unstable weather. The city lights grew brighter. I clearly saw the necklace of floodlights around the perimeter of the airfield. The lower we descended, the happier I felt. In less than a minute we would be on the runway; we were seconds away from safety.

Suddenly, with a gut-wrenching jerk we dropped out of the sky. The plane shuddered, and every metal part shrieked in protest as it hit the tarmac. A strange roaring noise exploded in my ears; the plane rocked crazily from side to side, creaking and straining in every joint.

It was all over in seconds, seconds that seemed like hours. With a final shuddering creak, the plane jerked to an abrupt stop, thrusting my body against the restraining seat belt. The pilot shut off all the electrical equipment and headed for the door. He shouted at us: "Quick! We've got to get out!"

The pilots forced the door open, and as I lunged toward it, my host said, "Grab your music." I won't pretend that I was cool, calm, and collected. I felt as panicky as the others looked. I grabbed my music and scrambled out of the plane as fast as I could. Then we ran, fearing an explosion. We dashed through the rain to what we judged was a safe distance before we dared look around to see what was happening. There was no sign of fire, although the searchlight's yellow fingers probed the dark, and sirens shrieked as airport fire trucks raced toward the wreck.

A huge jet about to bear down our runway for takeoff awkwardly backed up as it was rerouted to another runway. Still nothing happened to the dark shape that had been our Cessna 404.

My host lifted his left arm and maneuvered his wrist-watch into the searchlight's beam. "It's 6:40," he said. "The concert is due to begin at seven. There's nothing we can do here. We may as well go."

The roar of the rerouted jet blasted my ear drums, and I shivered as we picked our way through the rain. I recalled what a pilot had once said to me: "It's always better to be down here wishing you were up there, than to be up there wishing you were down here."

One of the security men drove by and offered us a ride to Butler Aviation. As soon as we got there, I went to the nearest pay telephone and phoned Linda.

"Honey," I said. "I've just been in a plane crash."

The line was silent for a second, and then Linda said, "Are you serious?"

"Yes, honey. You know I wouldn't joke about a thing like that. Our plane crashed here at Spokane, but, thank God, we're all alive."

It was seven o'clock by the time we reached the hotel, and the program began fifteen minutes later. To me that program was one of the most spiritual and memorable I have ever done. God's protecting care was so real to me that I felt like a Daniel delivered from the jaws of death.

The next morning I boarded another plane and flew back to Seattle. The Federal Aviation Administration investigated the crash and found that our pilot had forgotten to put the landing wheels down. Fortunately for us the wet conditions acted like grease on the tarmac and helped the plane's belly to slide along with less damage than would have ordinarily been the case. The rain also doused any spark that could have ignited leaking fuel and sent the plane up in a ball of flames. Oh, God, how great thou art!

> *The ultimate measure of a person*
> *is not where they stand*
> *in moments of comfort and convenience,*
> *but where they stand*
> *at times of challenge and controversy.*
>
> Martin Luther King, Jr.

♪

Chapter 27

Singing for the Governor

As I have said before, when God fulfills dreams, he often does it in ways that are "immeasurably more than all we ask or imagine" (Eph. 3:20). Several years ago I was asked to sing at a function in Birmingham, Alabama. On the appointed evening I was standing in the foyer of the convention center, waiting for the organizers to finalize the arrangement of the platform party. I didn't know most of the people milling about, but I conversed briefly with a few people I knew and then waited for the function to begin.

Then I saw security people near the door begin to scurry around, and above the hum of conversation, I heard the murmur, "The governor is coming. The governor is coming."

So the governor would be on the platform too. I straightened my tie and checked my suit as the governor walked in. It was Governor Bill Clinton, but I did not know that. His was not a familiar face at that time.

The ushers brought him across to where the rest of us were standing, and he was placed beside me. We shook hands, and although no one had introduced us, we fell into conversation while we waited.

Naturally, because we were in Birmingham, Alabama, and because I didn't know who he was, I assumed that he was the governor of Alabama. I began a long eulogy about Alabama. I told him how much I appreciated the natural beauty of the state and the friendliness of the people and that I had attended Oakwood College in Huntsville and so on.

The governor listened politely, a rather quizzical smile on his lips. He nodded as my enthusiasm for Alabama waxed more eloquent, but before he could reply, we were ushered on to the platform, and our conversation ceased.

As the program progressed and the introductions were made, I realized that the man to whom I had been talking was not the governor of Alabama but the governor of *Arkansas*.

I found no opportunity that evening for apologies or explanations. He spoke. I sang. Afterward we were both caught up talking to different groups of people, and eventually we went our separate way. I shrugged off the matter and hoped that it was such a small incident that he would forget all about it.

About four months before the 1992 elections, I met up with Governor Clinton again. By this time I knew who he was, so I decided I had better try to make amends. As we shook hands, I said, "Sir, you probably won't remember me, but we have met before."

He smiled and looked me in the eyes. "Yes, I do. You sang for me a year ago in Birmingham, Alabama."

I was shocked. "Governor Clinton, how could you remember that?"

He chuckled. "How could I forget it." Before we could pursue the matter further, an aide hurried him off to speak to someone else. I was amazed at his memory. All my hopes that he would not recall my faux pas were dashed.

Then in February 1993, I was invited to sing at the National Prayer Breakfast held in the ballroom of the Washington, D.C., Hilton. The guests had all been ushered to their places at the head table, and Linda and I were placed on the end, close to the door. For a few minutes we talked with the other people at the table, and then the doors opened and the conversational buzz that filled the great ballroom hushed as the announcer said: "Ladies and Gentlemen, the President of the United States." We all stood to our feet and applauded.

As President Clinton advanced into the room, I was the first person he saw. He threw his arms wide and stepped toward me, exclaiming; "Wintley, my friend."

In front of the television cameras and that huge gathering of people, he came forward and embraced me. I introduced him to Linda, and then he took his place at the table.

The program progressed as planned, and when it was time for me to sing, I walked up to the microphone and told the audience the circumstances of my first meeting with President Clinton and how I had mistaken him for the governor of Alabama. Roars of laughter rang around the room, and I had to wait until the clapping died down before I could begin to sing "God Bless America." As I returned to my seat, I passed the president again. He laughed and shook his head at me, whispering, "I can't believe you actually told these people how we met."

Then it was his turn to speak, and before he began his prepared speech, he said; "It was so nice to hear Wintley tell about our first rather awkward meeting. But what Wintley doesn't know is that I was ready to impersonate the governor of Alabama just to hear him sing."

Again the assembly laughed and clapped. I was struck by the incredible warmth and sincere affection that President Clinton had unabashedly demonstrated.

Several weeks later President Clinton sent a note telling that he enjoyed my music at the prayer breakfast. He signed it

simply, "With thanks, Bill Clinton, Governor of Alabama."
What a great sense of humor!

> *If I had permitted my failure,*
> *or what seemed to me at the time a lack of success,*
> *to discourage me, I cannot see any way in which*
> *I would ever have made progress.*

Calvin Coolidge
The Autobiography of Calvin Coolidge

♪

Chapter 28

God and Your Dreams

One night not long ago, I had a stark, vivid dream. In my dream, I was a little boy again, no more than four or five years old, and I was frolicking alone in a garden of aromatic flowers, skipping through blossoms aflame with color. I knew again the solace I had found only in my childhood dreams, and I didn't want to let it go.

Suddenly, I felt a gentle tap on my shoulder. It was unlike any touch I had ever felt, full of love and authority. I knew instinctively it was the Lord.

"You find sweet pleasure in your dreams of yesterday," he said. "Come with me. Let me show you my garden. Let me show you the future I have prepared for you."

He put his arms around me and led me to a garden where, as far as my eye could see, pure white, thornless roses grew. Each petal, perfectly sculptured, spoke of the love and care with which he nurtured every rose. What a sight it was. His garden!

"Look at my flowers," he said, as he motioned over that garden of pristine beauty. "Each rose holds a dream I carry in my heart for each of my children. One of these roses is for you."

Then he reached down, plucked the most beautiful rose I had ever seen, and gave it to me. As I held it, I felt so blessed, so fortunate, not just because of the gift, but because I knew it came from the hand of the King, the royal monarch of the universe.

"Son," he said, as I firmly clasped his gift, "hold this rose close to your heart. It will give your life the sense of purpose I wish for it to have. Wintley, I have a dream for your life, but it's up to you to believe that I can make it come true."

Then his voice became deeply earnest and filled with caution. "Listen carefully, my son. Unfaithfulness and sinful habits can cause you to forfeit the future I have prepared for you. Don't let sin defile the beauty of your future. This thornless white rose is a sign of the promise I make with you. Soon I am coming again for you and this rose. And I want you to be ready to return with me to your heavenly home."

As he spoke, I could almost feel that moment when we would stand together before the mansion he has prepared for me. What a precious moment it will be when I kneel on heaven's soil and plant my rose in that sacred place. There I will plant my dreams firmly in the fertile soil of heaven, where I will hear no echoes of doubt and confusion and where I will become exactly what he wants me to be.

"Oh," I whispered, "if only I could keep this dream alive."

He whispered back, "You can, with my help."

Did you know that God is a dreamer?

The original visionary.

When he dreams, constellations are born.

When he dreams, stars twinkle in the sky.

When he dreams, flowers ooze out of the ground and when they behold His glory they blush—in technicolor.

But did you know that when God the father dreams, he also dreams about you, his child? Did you know that he has a plan, a dream for your life?

The power in God's dream for you is limitless. To see that dream and act upon it can change your immediate physical circumstance, even mold and alter your destiny. Nothing can stand in the way of a dream birthed in the mind of God.

Take from his hand your dream, your white rose. And trust his plans for you. "'For I know the plans I have for you,' declares the Lord, 'plans to prosper you and not to harm you, plans to give you hope and a future'" (Jer. 29:11).

God has a dream for you. It's up to you to fit into his plan. God will even use miracles to make your dreams come true. God's plans for your life are far beyond the limitations of your mind.

I hope this book clearly illustrates that only when you surrender your dreams to God can you find the true fulfillment of those dreams. When you put your life into God's hands and let him take charge, your dreams become absorbed by the dream that God has for you. God makes himself responsible for your success and for making your dreams come true. When you give yourself and all that you are into God's hands, then you can expect to see wonderful things happen.

Let me share with you some principles God has taught me about his dreams for us.

HAVE A PURPOSE

If you want to succeed in life, you must have a goal, a dream, a sense of purpose. Together they will give direction to your life.

If you are not aware of your life's direction, ask yourself some questions. What is it that you most like to do? Probe into your mind. Find out what you most like doing and then dream about cultivating that gift.

Do you like to play baseball? Are you good at it? Then make up your mind to be the best baseball player in your school, in your town, in your state.

Are you fond of sketching? Do you dream of one day becoming a famous artist? You can be if you put your mind to it and work hard.

Those who pursue their dreams develop new talents. Those who bury their dreams stunt their growth.

BE WILLING TO WORK

Wishing and dreaming alone will not get you anywhere. You must be willing to work to make your dreams come true. Never allow "It can't be done," or "We've never done it that way before," to get in the way of your dreams. Obstacles are made to be overcome. Press on.

Some months ago I met a dreamer from India. When Harish was a small boy, he saw his neighbor's British passport. Harish was immediately fascinated by the occupation listed in the passport: printing. The words were scripted in the most elegant printing that Harish had ever seen.

He held the passport for as long as the neighbor allowed and gazed at the printing, trying to impress on his mind every curved line and every flourish that made the printing style so outstanding. At that moment a dream was born, a dream that someday he too would be a printer and would print like that.

Pens and paper were scarce in Harish's home, used only for serious study, not for dreamy little boys to practice printing fancy flourishes. But this did not discourage Harish. At every opportunity he dashed down to the nearby river bed, and with a pointed stick he traced letters in the wet sand. He wrote plain letters, and he wrote fancy letters. He practiced script alphabets and alphabets with all types of added flourishes. Hour after hour he wrote and drew and experimented with his letters in the sand.

Harish knew, without having to be told, that he must work to put foundations under his dreams. So, like all serious dreamers, Harish did his part to make his dreams come true. He studied hard and did the best he could at his school lessons, particularly making sure that his writing and printing were of copybook standard.

After Harish finished school, he worked at a printing establishment—but not as a printer. First Harish only swept the floors, washed the ink-smudged machinery, and trundled heavy rolls of paper around. It was a long time before he was allowed to try his hand at any printing.

For years Harish worked and watched and learned all he could about the printing processes and the paper trade. Now Harish owns the second-largest printing establishment in a beautiful country in the South Pacific. He knows that dreams come true if you do your part.

KEEP CLIMBING

As you work to fulfill your dream, you will face many obstacles. Many things will not work out the way you expect. But remember that nothing worthwhile is ever gained easily and without disappointments.

John James Audubon, the great artist-naturalist, one day left open the window of his room. A stray breeze blew the drapes aside and sent a sheaf of his intricately executed bird paintings fluttering to the floor. When the housekeeper came to clean the room, she assumed that Audubon had discarded the paintings scattered about the floor, so she swept them up and put them in the fire.

You can imagine Audubon's horror when he discovered what had happened. He could easily have given way to despair at having years of hard work destroyed. He could have ranted and raved at the ignorant housekeeper and dismissed her. He could have blamed God for sending the breeze into the room.

John Audubon did none of those things. Instead, he set about painting his bird pictures again. His heart must have been saddened by the loss. He must have wondered why such a calamity happened. But he did not waste time blaming anyone. Instead, he set to work to make good the loss.

What a lesson. When you are tempted to give up, keep climbing.

KEEP ON CLIMBING

God placed a dream in your heart,
And if you will make a start,
He wants for you to know
All of your needs he will supply.
He's always standing by;
He's there to see you through.
So keep on climbing until you reach your goal,
Keep on striving with all your heart and soul,
All things are possible with God.
So don't give in, he'll move your mountains.
He believes in your dreams.

People who are truly driven by a dream see failure as a temporary setback and not the final verdict. Every breakthrough in science, medicine, and the arts began with a dream. But don't forget how many failures preceded the fulfillment of these dreams.

Think of Thomas Edison, who eventually gave us the electric light bulb. His experiments failed repeatedly. Some people might have become discouraged and given up, but not Edison. He had a dream. A news reporter once said to Edison, "Why are you continually experimenting? You must have tried at least ninety times to make an incandescent light bulb. What are you accomplishing by all this? Surely it is just a waste of time."

Thomas Edison thought for a moment before replying, "It's not exactly wasted time. I have now discovered ninety ways that do not work."

What an insightful response. For fifty years Edison worked and experimented and dreamed. During his lifetime he took out patents for 1033 new inventions. We all know and use the outcome of Edison's work, and we are grateful that he kept on trying.

George Washington Carver, born a slave in the deep South, dreamed of bettering his people's agricultural methods. He studied and worked and experimented for years, surmounting setback after setback in his struggles to attain his dream. Eventually he taught his people to get the best from their soil by using crop rotation. He worked in his humble laboratory until he learned how to use the resulting prolific peanut crops in three hundred different ways. Every time you eat a slice of bread spread with peanut butter, think of George Washington Carver and his dreams.

You are never too old or too young to dream. Remember, if setbacks assail you, never take no as a final answer until God himself says no.

ADVICE TO PARENTS

If you are a parent, you can play a vital part in helping your children fulfill their dreams. First, you can lead your children to God, the person who holds the white roses for your children. Only when they know him and surrender their lives to him can they begin to dream about his dreams for them. If your children do not have an interest in God at this point, don't give up. I hope that my story reminds you that God can use many people and circumstances to bring us to himself. Pray for your children. Trust God's goodness.

Teach your children about God. And the best way to teach them is by example. All the "telling" in the world falls on deaf ears unless it is backed up by "showing." If you want your children to be loving, then show them love. If you want your children to be honest, then practice honesty. Parents are young children's major role models.

Listen to your children. Ask them what they like to do and why they like doing it. Ask whom they admire and ask why they admire that person. If you find that your children seem to have no particular aim, then expose them to other dreamers.

Inspire your children. Read to them. Read the Bible to them. Choose a translation that they will understand, and read them Bible stories from the Old and New Testaments. Show them that Jesus loves them and wants them to love him. Read other books to them. Choose inspiring biographies that are written especially for children. Read to them about George Washington Carver, Eli Whitney, Ben Carson, Abraham Lincoln, and Harriet Tubman. Help them see how ordinary young people were propelled by dreams that led them into exciting and productive lives of service to others.

Talk to your children. Tell them about your dreams for them. One mother nightly influenced her young son's dreams. When Eric Hare was a little boy, he went through a whole gamut of dreams and ambitions. Sometimes he wanted to be a firefighter and ride on the red fire engine and pull the rope that rang the bell. Sometimes he wanted to be a train driver or a stoker shoveling coal into the boiler's gaping maw. At other times he wanted to be a soldier and go off to war, firing his imaginary gun at imaginary enemies.

His mother just smiled and listened to his chatter. She never argued with him. She never pointed out that being a fire-fighter included more dangerous duties than riding on a red fire engine and ringing a bell. She merely smiled and listened. When bedtime came around, she said, "Come along now, Eric. Say your prayers, and I'll tuck you into bed."

So little Eric knelt down beside his bed and repeated after his mother: "God bless Mummy and Daddy; God bless my sisters and brothers; God bless my grandma and grandpa and keep us all safe." Then just before he finished, his mother said "God bless Eric. And when he grows up, make him a missionary for you."

Obediently little Eric repeated, "God bless me. And when I grow up, help me to be a missionary for you. Amen."

Night after night, week after week, month after month, until he was old enough to say his prayer unaided, little Eric repeated, "God bless me and when I grow up help me to be a missionary for you."

Is it any wonder that Eric grew to become a dedicated missionary in Burma?

Parents have power to influence their children's dreams. The mother of Ben Carson, a prominent neurosurgeon, is a prime example of this. Although she was a single parent who worked as a housekeeper to keep food on her table, Ben's mother urged her sons to read and study and excel at school, to prepare themselves for a special lifework, whatever it might be. "You can do anything that anyone else can do," she told them. "Only you can do it better. Keep at it." Her story, told in *Think Big* by Ben Carson and Cecil Murphy, is one of determination and self-sacrifice as she helped her sons fulfill their dreams.

Think back in history to the famous mothers who inspired their children to dream. Think of Abraham Lincoln's stepmother or Susannah Wesley, mother of John and Charles Wesley, or Whistler's mother. You too can inspire your children. Teach them. Listen to them. Encourage them. Read to them. Believe in them.

OLD WORDS TO YOUNG PEOPLE

If you are a young person, you can learn to dream. Remember that there is a world of difference between wishing and dreaming. Wishers usually sit back and wish and do nothing to help make their wishes come true. Dreamers dream, but they also work to make their dreams come true. Wishers will probably never get beyond wishing, but dreamers who combine their dreams with work will attain their goals.

Don't be afraid of work. In fact, don't settle for anything less than the best. We hear a lot about excellence these days. This new-found pursuit of excellence is often driven by a need for profits and by fear. Suddenly excellence, doing your best and being the best, has become the new rallying cry.

But as Christians we have not only a different motive for excellence but also a different standard of excellence. True excellence is not measured by greater profits and increased dividends; it is not measured by market shares and customer satisfaction. Our motive and standard for excellence is the Lord Jesus Christ. His life and his character is our standard of excellence. Christ is our pattern, our model, the yardstick by which we measure true excellence and all excellence is found in him.

True excellence is determined not by a person's career and achievements but rather by the person's possession of the virtues of Christ. We who are Christians have a unique calling and commitment to excellence. Because of our love for Jesus;

we are called to strive to reach the highest standards of excellence.

Remember, God's dream for you is more than comfort, success, or earthly security. God's ultimate dream for you is to become more like his Son, Jesus Christ.

Develop your talents. Cultivate what is noblest in yourselves, and be quick to recognize the good qualities in others.

As you work to make your dreams come true, be prepared to sacrifice to see your dreams come true. The mountain top cannot be reached by standing still and wishing yourself there. You can gain your object only by taking one step at a time, advancing slowly perhaps, but holding every step gained.

If you are a young person of commitment, if you have dreams that you want to see fulfilled, choose your companions wisely. Spend time with people who love God. Choose to be with people who respect God's dream for you. When you choose your heroes and role models, choose people of integrity, people who have worthwhile purposes in life, people whose dreams are guided by God's plan for them. Beware of people who are willing to sacrifice God and family in pursuit of their dreams. Beware of dreamers who cannot seem to break bad habits that harm their health and their spiritual welfare. Beware of peope who depend on drugs or alcohol or tobacco or any other harmful substances, while chasing their dreams.

Keep money and possessions in perspective. Although the world shouts that money and fame will bring you fulfillment, don't believe the lies. Wealth and fame are fleeting pleasures, at best. The only lasting joy comes from following God's dream for you.

Dear young person, God has a white rose for every one of you. Take that rose from his hands and aim high. There is no excellence without great labor. Make the most of your talents. Improve to the utmost every present opportunity. Close your ears to the voice of pleasure.

Have you seen the dream God dreams for you? That dream is the secret key that unlocks your identity and gives your life a sense of purpose and continuity. The dream that God dreams for your life is different from the dream that God dreams for any other life. He tailors every dream to fit the dreamer; and he does not give your dream to anyone else.

As you grow to attain your dreams and goals, remember this: to follow your dream you will need

> **D**etermination
> **R**esourcefulness
> **E**ndurance
> **A**spirations
> **M**otivation

May God bless you all and help you to attain your dreams.

VISION

One day Michelangelo saw a block of marble that someone had cast aside as having no value. "This piece of marble is valuable to me," said Michelangelo. "I see an angel imprisoned in it, and I must work to set the angel free."

Michelangelo had vision.

Vision is grasping with your heart what your intellect cannot comprehend. Vision is looking farther than you can see. Vision is believing in what you cannot prove.

Vision is what keeps you an original in a world of copies and facsimiles. Vision is the spark of divinity that turns over the engine of new possibilities in your life.

Vision is the hand of God pushing back the curtains of night so that dawn can rise on our apathy and indecision. Vision is an idea transplanted from the mind of God to the mind of his children. Vision is the ability and the audacity to dream the dreams of God. Vision is the only bridge that leads from the present to your future.

God has dreamed a dream for your life. It is a bright and wonderful dream. If you can only see it, it would burn your eyes. It is a dream of triumph and selfless service, a dream that you will spread his light and love to every nook and cranny of the world with which he has given you influence.

The power in the dream God dreams for you is stronger than the weight of tradition, mightier than the force of history. The right kind of dream can liberate an entire nation or emancipate a life from any negative circumstances.

The power to dream is the way to fulfillment and peace. Dreams are like keys that open life's locked doors. As you seek each day to fill your imagination with the exciting possibilities of God's will for your life, you will also fill your heart with wisdom, power, and the reality of his presence.

When you are living the dream God dreamed for you, fulfillment will come not from the applause of people but from the confidence that your life is centered in God's irresistible will.

To see your dreams come true requires decision, sincere purpose, watchfulness, and constant dependence upon God. Relinquish all claims on your life. Give everything you are and have to him, then stand back and watch your dreams come true. He has promised that if you find your delight in the will of the Lord, he will give you the desires of your heart. If your heart then has no desires and he has promised to give the desires of your heart, what then can God give you and still be true to his word and his promises? Dream the dreams of God, and all heaven will stand behind the power of that dream.

Wintley Phipps